I0100053

WHEN

TIME

WARPS

Finding Courage at the Right Time

ABSTRACT

Sam learned about the bully living inside him early in his life—that unwelcome voice that tried to define him. With Jessie's help, he also learned how to outwit it. As his mentor and friend, Jessie was one of the people who anchored Sam to what is important in life. Like Sam and most every other human on the face of the planet, if you are challenged by negative self-talk, this book is for you.

Bonnie Hedrick and Robert Canning

This book is dedicated to all those who struggle daily with emotional and physical pain.

And to those who do the small things every day to bring them hope.

And to the Jessies who decide to make a difference in their fragile life. I am blessed to have had many.

And, most especially to my children: Kristen Leopold and Robb Hedrick. May you always see yourself as someone truly special, someone to respect and believe in, someone to care about and love.

Table of Contents

Preface

"A snowflake begins to form when an extremely cold-water droplet freezes onto a pollen or dust particle in the sky. This creates an ice crystal. As the ice crystal falls to the ground, water vapor freezes onto the primary crystal, building new crystals—the six arms of the snowflake."[1] Even though all snowflakes are white and cold, they each have a different pattern and shape "because each one falls from the sky on its own path, thus encountering slightly different atmospheric conditions along the way."[2]

Like a snowflake, each person's journey on earth is unique, each one accumulating a multitude of experiences along the way—some of them good and some of them not so good.

Life events come in various shapes and sizes, with varying degrees of knocks and bumps, joy and accolades, or even shame and embarrassment. These can be mundane daily happenings, defining moments, or something more catastrophic.

As we breathe air on this planet, we interact with the universe and all living things with which we share it. We go to bed and get up. We do the things that are necessary to keep our bodies clean and nourished. We interact with animals and humans. As we go about our day, these daily tasks become habitual or rote. They only impact us negatively when a routine goes awry. For example, if something gets stuck between your teeth and makes your gum sore, your daily mundane task of brushing and flossing no longer happens without thinking. You attend to it cautiously and with care, and if all else fails, you seek the care of a dentist.

A defining moment, on the other hand, is "an event or time that shows very clearly what something is really about."[3] In a Huffington Post article, in January 2017, Jon Westenberg,[4] a contributing columnist, wrote, "Every life is a series of defining moments. Moments that shape and change us, and have a huge impact on our development and our choices....the first time I had my heart broken; the first time I worked for a day's wage; the first time I drank too much and made an ass of myself"[5] Defining moments are usually associated with intense feelings. They are seemingly unimportant, nevertheless, important moments that make them hard to forget.

Also, there are life events that are more life shattering or have the potential to be. In any given moment on any given day, life as we know it can be threatened or shattered. It only takes one event—a freak accident, a cancer diagnosis, a failed grade, a lost job, a broken home—to change our charted course. These potentially disastrous life events can happen quickly without warning and without regard for status, gender, age, or race.

When they happen in the first quarter of our lives, it alters the way our brain develops, and it can impact our health and well-being for life. The early years of a child's life are critical, because this is the period in life when the brain develops most rapidly, laying the foundation for health and wellbeing throughout life. The people we encounter, the messages we receive, the opportunities we have (or don't have) to learn—all of these life experiences accumulate, often converging and colliding to create our capacity for social, emotional, cognitive, and physical well-being—however functional or dysfunctional.

According to research, some adverse experiences are more harmful than others. They center on a parent's absence and/or neglect through death, divorce, incarceration, mental illness, and addiction; or through an adult's intentional physical, sexual, or emotional abuse of them. The adversities that are chronic or severe create the most toxicity and, therefore, the most destruction on our bodies over time.[6]

When catastrophic events happen in adulthood, our capacity for rational thinking is challenged. Our coping skills and peace of mind are harder to find. It is during these times that we need supportive relationships more than ever because time (our reality) seems to warp. The lives we have grown used to—taken for granted—become surreal and our altered reality is consumed with treatments, pain, and laden with emotional turbulence. That which has held us together may become translucent, even transparent; we find ourselves drifting off course, without purpose, and sometimes without the will to survive.

When time warps, it can seem like we're living in a parallel universe. Our altered reality might be consumed with having to adjust to new living circumstances, loss of job, riddled with medical appointments. The emotional turmoil underlying all of it can be debilitating.

Slipping into a time warp serves as a kind of spiritual (not ego) defense mechanism enabling us to cope with our frailty and vulnerability. During this time, it is hard to think beyond the boundaries of SELF due to our new reality. Much like the stakes buttressing young trees, we need family, friends, and internal fortitude more than ever to hold us up and help us return to our living.

Throughout Sam's story you will see how he learns to navigate his life's journey. Maybe what he learns can help you as well.

Chapter 1: Silver Linings

Sam and his family had crossed the Roebling Suspension Bridge many times as they travelled to visit his grandmother in Covington. That day in 1975, Sam was watching a big barge move slowly down the Ohio River beneath him, *kind of like my life*, he thought. The family's over-loaded station wagon crossed over the Roebling Suspension Bridge into Kentucky.

His mom's new job in Covington was uprooting him from the only home he had ever known.

Even though school, in general, was not one of his favorite places, he had made lots of friends at his school in Over-the-Rhine. Sam thought the best thing about school was playing with his friends at recess. Otherwise, school had too many rules, too much homework, and too much hard stuff to learn. For Sam, school was about friends. *And now I'll probably never see them again*, Sam thought as the Blue Goose made the Roebling sing.

In his Cincinnati school, he was one of the few white kids, but it didn't seem to matter. Everyone got along. One of his school buddies was an African American boy named Jerome. They lived next to each other and often played together after school. When the family's car pulled away from the curb on moving day, Sam saw Jerome standing in his bedroom window and waving goodbye, making the move even harder for Sam.

As the "Blue Goose," the family's big, clumsy, very blue station wagon moved across the "singing bridge,"[7] Sam could barely hear its song — something that Sam had enjoyed often as they crossed it to visit his grandmother. The rattling boxes in the back of the wagon grated on his nerves — Sam thought he was going to explode. His thoughts about leaving his friends and going to a new place were making as much noise in his head as the stuff in the back of the wagon. And they were causing him to feel terrible.

Finally, the "Blue Goose" turned onto Lee Street. It rolled up in front of his new home. *Same old, same old!* Sam thought. *Another apartment in another row house!*

As Sam stepped out of the wagon and onto the sidewalk, he was standing right in front of a narrow walkway that separated the houses. The concrete sidewalk stretched from building to building and for the entire length of the house. *It looks like a tunnel,* Sam thought. For a ten — almost eleven — year-old boy, it looked miles long and very scary — full of unknowns about a new home, a new school, and new friends.

As Sam stood looking down the tunnel, his mom joined him. "What do you think about our new place, Sam?"

"It kind of looks like our old street," Sam replied in an attempt <u>not</u> to appear too disgruntled.

"Yes, it does. See that market?" his mom asked as she pointed toward the family-owned grocery on the corner. "You'll be able to walk there. I used to go there when I was about your age."

Well, whoop-de-do! Sam thought. But he simply said, "Cool."

Sam's mom replied, "I think you'll like this neighborhood. It's quieter with fewer people and fewer cars than where we lived in Cincinnati. See that young girl riding her bike. Maybe you could get a bike too!"

Sam's ears perked up when his mom said that. He glanced toward his mom to see the expression on her face. He wanted to make sure he was hearing what she said. *Wow,* thought Sam. *A bike! That would be fun. And that would be different! Mom would never let me ride a bike in Over-the-Rhine.* But he remained defiantly unwilling to show any spark of enthusiasm.

About that time, a pickup truck overflowing with their furniture arrived, and right behind it was a car with some friends of Sam's grandmother. Gram, as Sam called her, was with them. *Thankfully,* Sam thought, *some people to help carry stuff.*

For Sam, a home was an apartment, usually in a row house and usually on the top floor. Row houses were tall, narrow houses that had been built in the heart of the city by German and Dutch families in the early 1900's. They were usually several stories high, one room wide, and about three or four rooms deep. Over time, as the families who owned them moved to the suburbs, the new owners converted the row houses to apartments. This would be the third one Sam had lived in since he was born.

He couldn't remember the first one. It was the apartment where his family lived when he was born. Even though he couldn't remember it, he had seen lots of pictures of his mom and dad with Jenna, his older sister. It was in that home that Jenna gave Sam his nickname, Sabbie.

Dutifully, Sam grabbed a box of his stuff from the Blue Goose and headed down the tunnel toward the entrance to the third-floor apartment. As Sam walked through the tunnel, he could only see a thin slice of sky above him. He felt like the walls were closing around him and he did not like it!

Once Sam reached the entrance he found the stairs that wound around and around, one floor after another till he reached the top. He thought he would never get to the top floor carrying his heavy box. When he finally arrived inside the apartment, he dropped the box to the floor, making a loud thud that echoed through the empty rooms. He was hot, tired, and disgusted!

His mom was already showing Jenna around the apartment; and when she heard the box hit the floor, she hurried to the entryway to find out what it was. "Sam! There are people below us. We have to be quieter than that!"

"It was heavy! I thought I'd never make it up those stairs." Sam replied with an irritated, almost angry, tone.

"Well, come with me and bring your box. I want to show you your new room." As they waked down the hall, she added, "Since you'll still need to share your bedroom with your brother, you can have the biggest one!"

Oh great! I get to share the room with Joey again! He can be so annoying. Why does Jenna always get a bedroom to herself? Sam grumbled in his mind as he begrudgingly followed his mom.

Their bedroom was a large room that was on the front corner of the row house. *Hmmm*, Sam thought as he looked it over. *Not bad.* Sam liked it because it had two large windows, one facing the street and one that looked off to the side. It also had a built-in bookshelf along one wall, next to the closet. *That's useful*, Sam thought as he dropped his box down next to the shelves.

"Sam! Please, stop that," his mom commanded. "The neighbors!" And with that directive, she left Sam to unpack his things. Since Joey was only six, Sam decided to let him have the bottom shelf, and he claimed the top three.

As Gram's friends began carrying the big furniture and more boxes labelled "SAM" into his room, Sam started unpacking them. He needed to see his things and get them settled around him as quickly as possible. He was busy placing books on shelves—actually, there were only three books—and clothes in dresser drawers when he heard yelling outside the side window. It was coming from a flat, oddly-shaped rooftop on the building that sat beside the row house.

On the roof, he saw an old man shouting at some boys. *Well, what on earth*! Sam thought. He watched the peculiar event unfold with as much suspense as he did any of his favorite TV shows.

"Scram," the old man yelled. "I told you to stay off my roof and to leave my birds alone!" Sam pressed his ear against the window—he didn't want to miss a thing! Then the old man started to chase the boys across the roof.

"Hey, old Indian, we're gonna kill those birds," yelled one of the boys as they laughed and ran all the way around a wall that apparently led to their escape route. Another one turned around to throw something at the old man.

Hmmm, Sam thought as he watched with wide eyes and open ears for any more action. *What will the old man do next*? But the old man just returned to a dilapidated shack and sat back in a lawn chair beside it.

Sam stood at the window for quite some time watching the mysterious old man as he puttered around his rooftop habitat. He watched him go in and out of the shack and wondered what the shack was used for. Sam actually whispered out loud, *I wonder if he lives there.*

A perfect campsite, Sam thought.

Another structure to the back of the shack looked like rusty, lopsided cages. They were tucked within a wooden frame that appeared to be made from the same discarded wood used in the shack. *I wonder what he keeps in those cages. The boys were talking about birds. Maybe that's where he keeps them*

Sam wondered about the old man. *Had the boys called him an Indian?* He was tall and stout, with white hair that he had pulled back in a ponytail. *He doesn't look much like an Native American; but then, I've never actually seen one,* Sam thought.

After a short while, Sam returned to the task of unpacking his things. He even helped unpack some of Joey's things. But that evening Sam was drawn back to the window when he noticed birds flying toward the cages. *So, he does have birds!* thought Sam. *They're probably pigeons.*

He watched as the old man greeted the birds. One by one, they landed on a perch near the cages. Then the old man held out one hand and one bird at a time flew to him. When it landed in his hand, he took his other hand and placed it over the bird's head as if concocting some magical spell over it. He paused a bit with each bird, held it high in the air, and then gently placed it in a cage. He wondered why the old man did this.

There was one bird that got more attention than the others. Sam watched the old man talking to it as if it were a long-lost friend. And then it happened! Sam saw the old man take a note off the bird's foot. *I wonder what that note says,* thought Sam. *I wonder who it is from. What is that old man up to?*

An old man, a rooftop campsite, and pigeons that carry notes! Sam had to get to the bottom of this mystery! *Maybe this place is not going to be that bad,* thought Sam as he stared out the window.

15

Chapter 2: Messages and Messengers

It didn't take long for Sam and Joey's bedroom to look like they had lived there for years. Everything had been put away, pictures were hung, and Joey's toys were usually spread across the floor. Bunk beds sat in one corner of the bedroom near the window where Sam had stood for hours watching the old man on the rooftop.

Sam had spent a lot of his free time watching the roof and anticipating more action; but the boys did not return. Most of the time, the old man was just fiddling with the bird cages, sitting in the sun in his lounge chair, or doing something in the shack.

Sam had tried to get up in the morning in time to see if the old man was writing notes for the pigeons to carry, but that never seemed to happen. It was summer, school was out, and he liked to sleep late. It didn't take long for that to change.

There it is AGAIN! Sam thought as he sat upright in his bed. "Why are you waking me up EVERY day?" Sam whispered with clenched teeth. He knew he needed to be quiet. He didn't want to wake Joey up too early.

The sound was that fluttering sound that birds make when they hover over something, and it was coming from his window. Every morning, he would climb down from the top bunk, run to the window to see the bird; but it was too quick and off it would fly. More than once, it left a feather teetering on the edge of the window sill.

Sam began to collect the feathers in a shoebox he kept on one of the top shelves in their room. On the outside of the box, he wrote in big letters, "HANDS OFF! THIS IS SAM'S." Joey, Sam's little brother, liked to get into his things; and Sam wanted to make sure he did not play with the feathers.

When Sam was younger, he had heard his mom and grandmother talking about how Joey couldn't do things as quickly as other kids his age. He had been slower to walk, feed himself, and talk. When Joey was four, the pediatrician referred him for testing. That was the year they found out Joey's ability to learn would peak at about age seven or eight. Sam tried to be patient with Joey for that reason, but sometimes he was just too bothersome. Sam knew if he didn't secure the box — maybe even hide it — that Joey wouldn't leave it alone.

Sam thought summer breaks always ended too soon, and the summer of 1981 was no different. Sam's first day of fifth grade in his new school had arrived. That morning he was awakened, as usual, by his early morning bird visitor. The nuisance had become almost as bothersome as Joey; and on that day, it was also an annoying reminder that he had to go into a new school, with no friends, and no idea where to go and when. Sam just turned over in this bed, pulled his pillow over his head, and tried to will it away.

"Up and at 'em," his mother yelled as she flipped on the light of his bedroom.

"Argh!" grumbled Sam.

"You have 30 minutes before we need to leave. That's time for you to dress and eat some breakfast. Gram will be here to take you to school by then," Sam's mom directed.

Obligingly, Sam threw the covers back and climbed off the top bunk. Joey was already up and in the kitchen. *How could he be that energetic this early,* Sam thought, as he moseyed to the bathroom.

On time, Sam and Jenna walked into Park Elementary with their grandmother and Joey. They went straight to the Principal's office. They were greeted by Mr. Spalding, the principal, and Ms. Freytag, the counselor. The principal suggested Ms. Freytag take Jenna to her office for orientation, and he asked Sam to sit down in a chair in front of his big desk. It was covered in papers — neatly stacked, and apparently, sorted by subject.

Mr. Spalding spent about a half hour with Sam giving him his schedule and a hand-drawn map of the building. He told Sam the name of his teacher and a little bit about what the class would be studying.

He also looked over Sam's file that had come from the other school. Apparently, he noticed the trips to the principal; and, he let Sam know that the school had rules and that each student was expected to follow them. He pointed to a list of rules that were mounted on his wall. Sam nodded in agreement throughout the 30 minutes, but did not have much to say — especially about rules.

Then Mr. Spalding walked Sam to his classroom. When they entered, Mr. Spalding greeted the class and introduced Sam to Ms. Fletcher, the teacher. Mr. Spalding then left to return to his office to work on something that was in one of the neat stacks of paper on his desk.

Ms. Fletcher showed Sam to his desk which was about half-way down the second row. The desks were lined up, six to a row; and, there were five rows. Sam looked across the faces of the students. It was different — not like his old school where he was only one of a few white kids. In Park Elementary, the students were mostly Caucasian with a few African American.

Sam listened to the teacher as she went over classroom rules, the daily schedule, and expectations about student behavior and academic work. It was school just like his old school, which meant Sam's mind wandered outside the windows and dreamed about doing something else — anything besides rules, math, or geography.

Awkwardly at lunch, Sam sat down by himself and began to eat something that looked like meatloaf with tater tots and green beans. Not long after he sat down, a boy sat down beside him.

"Hello, my name is Dave," said a boy with a big smile and frizzy, unruly hair the color of cinnamon. Sam looked the dude up one side and down another. He was not sure about what the boy might want.

"Hello," Sam replied as he gave Dave another look. Dave was smiling from cheek to cheek – the kind of smile that lightens trepidation. Dave's gentle introduction lightened Sam's reservation.

"Do you like the new school?" asked Dave.

"It's okay," replied Sam. "School is school, no matter where you go."

"I hear that!" Dave agreed. Their conversation about what they liked to do and a lot of other things continued through the entire lunch period. With that simple "hello" and friendly conversation, the ice was broken and Sam and Dave launched a friendship that would last for many years.

Not long after school began, Sam was given an assignment to do a book report for literature class. The report was due at the end of October. As part of the assignment, the teacher instructed the class to take notes on index cards — at least 20 notes — to use in writing the report.

He got the idea of connecting his assignment to what was happening each morning. The early morning wake-up call had persisted so long that Sam was determined to find out why. *Is the bird from the old man's flock? And why this window? There are lots of windows on this side of the row house,* Sam thought.

So, on one Saturday, Sam surprised his mother by asking to go to the library to get a book for the report. His mom knew that libraries, like schools, were not one of Sam's favorite places and she was more than happy to take him.

"That's great," she said. "When is your book report due?"

"It's due at the end of October, and I want to find a book about birds. Do we have any index cards?"

Sam's mom didn't question his motives; she was just happy to see his interest in going to the library. She found some cards and gave them to Sam to put in his book bag. Then she walked him to the library on Madison Avenue and gave him specific instructions to stay there until she returned from the market. "Take good notes," she said in a loud whisper as she left Sam by the front desk.

Since this was Sam's first visit to the Kenton County Library, Sam asked the librarian for help in finding books about birds. Mrs. Scott, the librarian, pointed to one section where he could find books specifically about different kinds of birds; and then she reminded Sam that he could always find information in the encyclopedias.

Sam didn't make it to the encyclopedias. In the section about birds, he found more books than he ever thought there would be! As he was perusing the shelves, he found a book on American Indian[8] myths and legends. The subtitle caught his eye — *Birds play a wide variety of roles in Native American culture.*[9] Sam started to put two and two together. *The boys on the roof called the old man an Indian and he keeps birds,* Sam thought. *This might help me understand what the old man is doing with those birds, and why one of them is coming to my window.* Since he had about an hour to kill before his mom returned, Sam decided to get started on the first chapter.

It didn't take long for Sam to realize the information in the book was way above his head. He couldn't read much of it; but he did look at the pictures and read the captions long enough to know that in Native American mythology, birds were viewed as messengers from the Creator. In other words, they acted as messengers between humans and the spirit world.

Sam's curiosity grew tenfold! He wondered if the spirit world was trying to tell him something with all these bird visits and feathers. The thought made him shiver. *But, who could it be and what do they want to say?* Sam thought as he felt the goosebumps crawling up his arms.

After Sam finished reading what he could about Native American mythology, he went to the youth section to see what he could find on birds. He still needed to find a book he could actually read for his book report, and he wanted to see if he could determine the kind of birds the old man was housing. *Are they pigeons?* Sam wondered.

He found a couple of books that he thought would be helpful. One was full of pictures of birds and feathers. In it, he found pictures of pigeons that he thought looked like the old man's birds. *They've gotta be!* Sam thought. *These pictures look just like them.*

Sam was excited to find lots of facts about pigeons in the other book he chose. That's when he decided his book report would not be on birds, in general, but on pigeons, specifically. He started to take some notes on his index cards:

- Pigeons weigh about nine pounds.
- The color of their feathers depends on their habitat and the type of diet.
- They have strong muscles and can fly 50-60 miles per hour.

The next paragraph in the book caused Sam to pause. He read about squab, the meat of young pigeons. *Do people eat them?* Sam questioned. The thought made him a bit nauseated, but he decided to make note of it and include it in his report.

- The meat of a young pigeon is called squab and people eat it.

Sam started to scan through more pages in the book. He wanted to know about the notes that pigeons carry — to whom and why they were written. He read about homing pigeons and rock pigeons in the book and was fascinated by the homing pigeons' ability to find their way home. He added:

- There are different kinds of pigeons and some can fly long distances and carry messages.
- Homing pigeons use low-frequency sound waves that come from the Earth's surface to mentally map a path back to their loft

Sam was so engrossed in his reading, that he didn't notice his mom come into the library. It wasn't until he felt his cap sliding over the top of his head and covering his face that he knew she was there.

"Are you about ready to go, Sam?" questioned his mom.

"I'd really like to take these books home. I'm not quite finished with my notes. Can we do that?" Sam asked.

"Sure, I'll help you get a library card," she responded, and they took the books to the counter. Mrs. Scott took his name and address and filled out some more information. Then, she presented Sam with a card that had his name on it. When Mrs. Scott handed Sam the card, she said, "Sam, this card enables you to go to any library branch in Kenton County to find information you might need, and check out books for enjoyment. You must use it responsibly, follow all the rules for taking care of the books you take, and return them on or before their due date."

Sam agreed and smiled with pride about being trusted with this new responsibility. All the way home, Sam could not stop chattering about how fast pigeons fly, how people eat their meat, and other things that did not interest his mother much.

Once home and back in his room, Sam thought about all this new information about pigeons; and he was even more curious about what the old man was doing with his birds. He still wanted to know if the pigeon that was visiting him each morning was from the old man's flock. *If it is, what is it trying to tell me?* Sam thought as he remembered the information about messages from the spirit world. That's when Sam decided it was time to meet the old man and maybe get some answers from him.

Sam knew the boys that the old man chased from the rooftop had disappeared behind the wall of a small out-building that was connected to the apartment building. Even though he couldn't see it from his window, he assumed there was an entrance to the roof somewhere beyond that wall. So, he decided that on the following Saturday, he would find the window or door that led to the roof.

He knew, though, that he had to talk to his mom about venturing onto an open roof and talking to a strange, old man. *If I don't, there will be grief, big grief!* Sam thought. *But when? She is so busy with her new job!*

23

Most of the time after school Sam and Jenna had to go to their grandmother's house until their mom got off work. Gram's small house was just around the corner on Main Street. That's why Sam and Jenna didn't understand why they couldn't just go to their own home! And their own room! After all, as Sam often argued, "I'm in the fifth grade now and Jenna is in the sixth. We are old enough to take care of ourselves and Joey too for that matter."

Regardless, their mom insisted on her mom watching over them. On warm, sunny days, Gram would walk them to their apartment at 5:00 PM when it was time for his mom to arrive. On one of those days when his mom came home from work, Sam took advantage of both his mom and his grandmother being in the apartment. He called them to his bedroom to look at the rooftop and get their permission for him to visit the old man on the roof.

"Mom, Gram, could you come here?" When they arrived, Sam was standing at the window. "Have you seen that old man on the roof? He has birds that live in those cages. I think they are pigeons, and I want to visit him to talk to him about the birds — for my book report," he quickly added.

"I don't know," said his mom. "What do you think Gram? Do you know anything about him?"

"I've never paid much attention to what was going on down there," Gram said as she paused to look over the old man's campsite. "Well, the roof looks safe enough. And I think the old man is Walter something, or maybe something Walters. He's been in the neighborhood a long time — I've seen him walking on the street and at the market."

"Hmmm, I think I know him!" Sam's mom said as she looked more closely at the old man. "I think he was the maintenance man at my elementary school. What could he possibly be doing living on the roof?"

"I have no idea!" Gram replied. "But, I think he is harmless enough."

"Can I visit him?" asked Sam trying to contain his excitement.

"Let me think about that Sam," his mom reluctantly responded. "It's been a long time since I knew him, and it is a big, open roof!"

The conversation ended with Gram excusing herself to go home and get ready for church. She went faithfully on Wednesdays and Sundays, and she liked for the family to go with her. Sam's mom, Gayle, was not as enthusiastic. But sometimes, Gram absolutely insisted that Sam, Jenna, and Joey go with her on Sunday morning.

Gram was an important part of the family and like a second mom to Sam and his brother and sister. She was also like their "tour guide" for the new neighborhood because she had lived there her entire life. As such, she was the first to warn Sam to steer clear of the hooligans that were running around the neighborhood causing trouble. "They are a group of boys about your age, Sabbie; and they are going to get in some serious trouble. You know 'Birds of a feather stick together.' I don't want my neighbors thinking you are one of those hooligans."

What? Sam thought. He didn't quite understand "feathers sticking together," but he did wonder if the boys he had seen on the roof were part of those "hooligans."

Sam had Jenna to thank for the nickname Gram used — Sabbie. When Sam was born, Jenna was almost two. When she tried to learn Sam's name, she got "Sammy" all mixed up with "baby;" and it came out "Sabbie." From then on, it just stuck like bubblegum on the bottom of his shoe. Most of the time, that's the name his family used for him. He didn't mind it too much when used by his family at home; but once he started school, he didn't want Jenna or anyone to use it in front of his friends.

25

Unlike Sam, Jenna never had any problems in school. She made good grades, got along with all the other girls, and was the teacher's little helper. Oh, yes, Jenna was perfect or so everyone thought! Her long brown hair almost reached her waist. Her eyes were crystal blue; "just like your dad's," Gram once said.

After Gram left to go to church and his mother started cooking dinner, Sam stood at his bedroom window to watch the birds come back to the roost. Like always, the old man greeted the birds and took the note from the foot of that one special bird. *You are a curious old bird yourself, Old Man,* Sam thought. *I will meet you soon and find out what is on that note!*

Chapter 3: Challenges

The scuffle happened in mid-October just before Sam's book report was due. It all began when Sam spied some cool looking hats on a rack in the shoe store on Madison Avenue. Sam and his cousin Troy were shopping for Troy's basketball shoes. Troy was sixteen and Sam thought he was AWESOME!

While Troy was trying on shoes, Sam began looking through the hats. Some had logos of sports teams. He was trying to find just the right one. He landed on a red one with white letters that read, "I'd rather be playing hooky." He placed the hat on his head and turned to Troy to get his reaction. Smiling from ear-to- ear, Troy took the hat off Sam's head, adjusted the cap size, and then placed it back on Sam's head along with a lifted hand for a high five. That was enough to convince Sam the hat was perfect!

"That hat is $2.75, Sam. Do you have enough money for it?" questioned Troy. Sam dug down into his pocket and first pulled out a white baggie. Troy almost laughed out loud when he saw the baggie, because he knew exactly what it was for and why Sam had it in his pocket. "Gram's got you walking Smokey now, right?" asked Troy.

"Oh yeah, every day after school!" Sam replied as he continued to dig in his pockets. He finally had two dollars and five dimes in his hands. Troy saw the disappointment on Sam's face when he realized he didn't have enough money. Troy had already anticipated that there might be a problem, and he had two quarters in his hand just in case. Placing them in Sam's hand, he said, "That should be more than enough."

"Thanks, Troy!" said a very appreciative Sam. With hat on head and feeling most satisfied with this purchase, Sam and Troy headed out of the store. As they were walking home, they saw a group of boys, maybe five or six, in a playground on Pike Street. They were throwing rocks at some pigeons causing them to squawk and fly away. Troy asked Sam if Gram had given him the lecture about "the hooligans."

"Oh yeah, that came early on. She said something about birds and feathers, but I didn't understand much of it." As they continued talking, Sam paused to pick up an interesting looking feather and stuck it in his pocket. Then, glancing back toward the boys, Sam said, "They don't look too tough."

"It's best just to steer clear of them, Sam. If they don't watch out, they are going to get in big trouble."

As they crossed over to Lee Street, Troy started talking about basketball and explaining some of the terms used in the game. "In basketball, Sam, 'assist' means to hand off the ball to the guy who has the best shot at the basket," Troy said. Then he made his point by using his "assist" with the purchase of the hat. Although Troy was only a few years older than Sam, in Sam's eyes he was an authority on how to be cool in fifth grade!

Troy was Sam's cousin on his mom's side of the family, and they had spent almost every holiday together since Sam was born. Troy lived in the same neighborhood in Covington, which made it convenient for Troy and Sam to hang out together sometimes.

As it turned out, Troy's "assist" from the shoe store ended up getting Sam in a lot of trouble. It wasn't so much what Troy did, but what Sam did with it.

Sam thought his hat was really cool so the very next day he wore it to school proudly. Ms. Fletcher, Sam's teacher, had a very different opinion about the hat, especially about the phrase on it. As soon as she noticed it, she asked Sam to take a seat on her three-legged teaching stool in front of the class. When he sat down on the stool, he removed the hat; but the teacher said, "Oh no, please leave the hat on, Sam." And then she turned to the class and said, "Let's talk about the saying on Sam's hat." And, that led to a class discussion about respecting education and obeying school rules.

As Sam sat on the stool, he felt the focus of fifty eyes on him. He even heard some of the kids snickering. His blood rushed up his neck turning his face a beet red. He wanted to run as fast as he could out of the classroom, down the hall, and out the front door of the school.

Finally, he heard the teacher say something about removing the hat and returning to his seat. The last thing he heard was, "Don't ever wear that disrespectful hat to school again, or I will keep it." Sam thought that was bad enough, but he found out that wasn't the worst of it when he got to the lunchroom!

Just as Sam sat his tray down on the long lunchroom table, Noah showed up with his friend Monty. Noah should have been in sixth grade, but he had failed a year. The age difference made him bigger than other kids in his class. Because of it, he liked to throw his weight around and make kids give up their seat in the lunchroom, or be the first to be picked for a game, or just to back down some kid for no reason at all other than just to be mean. Sam always tried to steer clear of him.

"Looky, looky, Sabbie's playing hooky!" scoffed Noah.

"Where'd you get that hat, Sabbie?" Monty chimed in. "Did your daddy give you that hat to go with that baby name?'

Noah couldn't let Monty have all the fun, so he blurted out, "Where is your daddy anyway?"

Before Sam knew it, his plate of spaghetti was flying toward Noah, and it landed across his face. Sam heard the clank of the plate as it hit the concrete floor. Noah just stood there like he was stunned. When the plate hit the floor, Sam felt Monty push him from behind. He quickly turned around and before either of them knew it, they were on the floor rolling in the spaghetti. That's when Mr. Spalding and Mr. Coates, the assistant principal, came through the door and grabbed all three of them and yanked them toward the principal's office.

After at least 30 minutes of lecture that included the disciplinary action, Mr. Spalding handed all three of them a note with stern instructions to take it to their parents and have it signed. It needed to be returned to him the following day. As they were leaving, Noah got close enough to Sam to whisper: "You better watch your back, Sam. This doesn't end here."

After school, Sam was sitting on a bench in front of the school waiting for Jenna. He was keeping an eye out for Noah and Monty. He didn't want any more trouble. As he was looking behind him, he saw James, another classmate, coming down the sidewalk. The smirk on James' face as he walked by confirmed what Sam had suspected — that, following the lunchroom brawl, kids had made fun of him all day. *They'll probably be laughing at me for a long time*, Sam thought. He just looked down and shuffled his feet in the gravel. *What a way to start a new school! Maybe this hat was not such a great idea*, Sam thought, as he wadded up the hat and stuffed it in his book bag.

When Jenna arrived at the bench, the first thing out of her mouth was, "Boy, are you in big trouble!" Then she challenged Sam to race home, but Sam was in NO hurry to get home given the note in his pocket and all! He just wanted to crawl in a place as far away from people as he could, and he wondered what Jenna's hurry was! *Probably to tell on me*, he thought.

Sam and Jenna walked to Gram's house, as usual, but when Sam finally got home, he went immediately to his room and climbed upon the top bunk. From his birds-eye view, he could see the rooftop easily despite the raindrops that had begun to form on the window pane. *I must surely be slow like Joey*, Sam thought. *Otherwise, why on Earth would I continue to get myself into these predicaments?*

Sam's woefulness was interrupted by a sound at his bedroom window. Quickly, Sam glanced over and saw that it was the bird that annoyed him so early each morning. He slid off his bunk and quietly approached the window. For the first time, he was eye to eye with his feathery friend. They stared at each other for a moment till Joey bounced into the room and scared it away.

"Joey!" Sam yelled. "Do you have to be so loud?" Startled by Sam's harsh tone, Joey left quickly; and Sam returned to his bunk to wallow in self-pity.

Sam had to admit to himself that it wasn't the hat that got him into so much trouble at school. It was what followed his teacher's reprimand that was the real problem. Painfully, Sam knew it was his runaway anger at lunch that caused the brawl. It seemed to happen a lot more since the move, even over silly things like Jenna taking too long in the bathroom or Joey leaving his toys on the floor of the bedroom.

Sam knew that he had to give the principal's note to his mother and give an account of what happened at school. This was not the first principal's note that Sam had ever delivered to his mom. There were several notes during his third and fourth grades about not paying attention in class, not completing homework, or getting into quarrels on the playground.   But this was the first note from his new school.

He was not looking forward to dinner! He stared out the window until his eyes stopped at the cages on the rooftop. The pigeons moving about and fluttering in their cages briefly distracted Sam from his anticipation of impending doom!

His mom's command to come to dinner snapped him back to reality. He hesitated until her voice reached a tone that meant he could postpone no longer. Sam wondered just HOW he should bring up the whole thing!

He didn't have to wonder long. The first thing out of Jenna's mouth was, "Sabbie got in trouble at school today."

Sometimes she could be the most irritating person on Earth! Sam thought. He tried quickly to explain that the teacher thought the saying on his hat was disrespectful and that she threatened to keep his hat if he ever wore it in her classroom again.

But, of course, that wasn't good enough for Jenna; and she had to add, "That's not what I'm talkin' 'bout! I mean at lunch!" in that whiny tone that was uniquely Jenna. Her words scorched through Sam's ears until they landed in his frontal cortex. Sam closed his eyes, thinking if he couldn't see her she might not be there.

The only thing that came to Sam's mind in that moment was the sound of pigeons screeching, wings a-flapping, and gray and white feathers flying everywhere, just as they had done when he saw "the hooligans" tossing pebbles at them in the playground on Pike Street.

Sam choked up a bit and started to tell his mom what happened. As he recounted the story, he looked at Jenna with a stare that could melt ice. "What I want to know is how they knew my nickname!" Jenna just shrunk down in her seat.

"What did you do, Sam?" his mom asked in a tone that reflected her dismay over what to do with an angry young boy.

Sam continued to explain, "I did the first thing that came to my mind with what I had. I threw my plate of spaghetti in Noah's face and wrestled Monty to the floor! And MOM, I bet my dad would have done the same thing, wouldn't he?"

But, like the principal who put Sam in detention for three Saturdays, his mom wasn't biting at this attempt to turn the conversation away from his lunch antics. After much discussion about right and wrong, sticks and stones, Sam was assigned to do the dishes for three weeks and to write an apology to the janitor for having to clean up the mess, the principal for making trouble at school, and the two boys — all before school the next morning.

Still, his mother would not say much about his dad! For whatever reason, she did not talk about where he went or why. He was just never there from the time Sam was about three years old. The only thing she ever told Sam was, "He just went away." Sam had even tried to get information from his grandmother and other relatives, but all anyone would ever say were things like: "Well, Sam, he went to war" or "Sam, the important thing is you have a mother who loves you." Never would anyone give him anything he could understand.

But Sam did have a vague memory of his dad taking Jenna and him to the park. He remembered the feeling he got when his dad picked him up and carried him on his shoulders. And he remembered the last time he left, in his brown uniform and a strange little hat tucked over his belt. And he remembered his crystal blue eyes. Like Jenna's, they were the color of a bright blue sky.

Chapter 4: Choices

Sam had been grounded for a week following the hat incident, but that was now behind him. His focus had shifted back to the annoying early morning bird visitor.

Each time the bird came to his window, Sam became even more determined to talk to the old man. Even though his mom had not made her decision about him going on the roof, he decided he couldn't wait any longer. So, one day after school, he ventured toward the second floor window hoping to find the entrance.

It didn't take long for him to find it. It was a large window on one of the short hallways on the second floor. The window had a latch at the top of the bottom pane, so Sam thought getting through it would be easy. But, still, it caused Sam to stop his pursuit and think about what would happen to him if his mother found out about his wanderings. He didn't want to be grounded again – or worse!

At the window, Sam surveyed the route to the old man's habitat. He would have to cross a narrow ledge along the roof's edge till he got to the open space where the old man lived. He couldn't see the ledge from his window so this, too, caused Sam some hesitation.

He could see the shack from the window, but he didn't see the old man. *Is he in the shack?* Sam thought. *Is it too dangerous? What could it hurt if I just went exploring? What will my mom do if she finds out? What if the old man is mean? What if the birds attack me?*

There is no doubt. These questions caused Sam to pause, but his curiosity won out! He thought surely an "old Indian" who lived on a roof would be willing to talk to a kid about his birds; and, more importantly, he might know about messages from the other side! So, cautiously, Sam decided to solve the mystery that lay beyond the window.

———

35

Okay, Sam thought, *this is no big deal. There's plenty of room to step onto the roof just below the window.* Once he was on the roof, though, he thought, *What the heck was I thinking?*

His uneasiness about breaking rules turned to butterflies in his stomach about being so high up and about approaching the old man. He decided to stick closer to the wall as he crept toward the corner. At the corner, he hesitated one last time. *Will mom see me from the apartment? What will I say to the old man if he IS there?* With one last moment of hesitation, he peeked around the corner. *Hmmm....no movement on the roof,* he thought. *Maybe I can get a closer look.*

Venturing into the open space on the roof, Sam looked toward the third floor of his apartment building. Which window was his? The kitchen? His mom's bedroom? *Hopefully,* he thought, *she won't be standing in one of them!*

Sam made his way to the old man's shack to get a closer look. He thought about what to say if the old man was there. When he got closer, he yelled out; but it came out more like a long drawn-out, loud whisper, "Hello, anyone there?" With no answer came a sigh of relief.

He first looked around the pigeon cages. No pigeons. He looked for pigeon food, questioning what on earth pigeons ate anyway to give them their distinctive colors. He found the food in a large burlap sack near the cages. The sack was full of seeds — many kinds that were different colors and shapes.

He made his way around the cages till he came to the makeshift door of the shack. He knocked on the faded wood that looked like it had been taken from a dumpster somewhere. *Hmmm, should I peek inside?* he thought. *Well, it's only a half door. It doesn't even have a doorknob.* So, he cracked it just enough to peek through the small opening.

When he saw a strange-looking wall hanging that looked like a wheel with lots of colorful feathers hanging from it, he had to get a closer look. He first stuck in his left foot and shoulder through the cracked door; but before he knew it, his whole body just slipped inside what he would discover to be a portal to the old man's soul.

He went first to the colorful wall hanging. He gently touched the network of string that looked like a spider web. It covered the entire opening of the circle. Dangling from the circle were several leather strings that were decorated with glass beads and feathers of all sorts and sizes. Sam had never seen anything like it.

After spending some time at the wall hanging, a collection of pictures and memorabilia posted on another wall caught his eye. The old man had made a display of old photographs on a board that had been framed with a painted yellow border. *Likely family*, Sam thought. But when he looked closer at the photos, several were men in Air Force uniforms. Some of the men were wearing bomber jackets with parachute sacks sitting in front of them.

There were also medals from the Air Force. One of the medals had a purple ribbon with a gold heart at the end. Sam had heard about a Purple Heart[10] medal but didn't know about its significance. He was still impressed, though, and wondered why the old man had one.

A military hat lay on a shelf beside the display board. The hat deserved a much closer look because it reminded Sam of the last time he saw his dad. This hat was flat with a creased, folded crown. It was dark green with gold stripes. Sam smiled as he ran his fingers across the gold stripes. He remembered his dad's hat. It was the same shape—flat, brown and neatly folded and tucked in his belt the day he left. Sam got a lump in his throat as he remembered that day.

Below the photos was a small table. On it were several pieces of paper and a couple of pencils with no erasers. There was also a spiral notebook titled, "The Science of Flight and Navigation." One of the notes was open and Sam could see writing on it. *Should I read it?* thought Sam but he could hardly keep from it. There were only four words: "Use your instruments wisely." *Who is it to or who is it from?* Sam wondered.

He then noticed a carefully folded blanket draped at the foot of an army cot that sat along one wall. Stacked beside the cot were books on aircraft navigation, Air Force magazines, and papers from the early 60's. There were bookmarks in some of them making Sam wonder if these sections were favorites of the old man. *I wonder why he is so interested in navigation,* thought Sam.

The guilt returned, and Sam became concerned. It felt like he was in someone's private sanctuary, and he knew he needed to get out and fast! He took one last look around and then headed toward the door. That's when the door started to open, very slowly. Sam knew he was trapped. He felt his blood draining from his body and out his toes. In the doorway was the old man. Sam gasped. The old man also stepped back a few steps and eyed his intruder from top to bottom.

The old man's white hair was pulled back off his tanned face. The expression on his face was stern and questioning. And, surrounding his furrowed brow were the signs of age and sadness. His clothes were clean but faded and old. *He's even scarier up close,* Sam thought as he felt his body grow small next to the tall, stout man.

He and Sam were locked in a stare that was only broken by the old man's aging voice. "Who are you? I ought to throw you off the roof right now! I told you boys to stay away!" he said as he took a step toward Sam.

Sam's heart stopped briefly as he anticipated the fall to the ground. He quickly said, "My name is Sab. I mean Samuel," as he managed to get around the old man and squeeze through the opened door, trying hard not to touch him. He was so close to the old man that he could hear his breathing. Then Sam pointed toward his apartment. "I live up there," he said timidly as he moved out of the man's reach.

"Well, get back up there," scolded the old man. "You are in my home!"

Sam nervously and quickly replied, "I'm sorry! I've never been here before. I've been watching you with the birds, and I'm curious about what you are doing."

"Well, curiosity killed the cat, kid! Now scram!"

Sam ran toward the second-floor window faster than pigeons ever took off from their cages. But when he got to the corner, he couldn't help but turn around and yell back toward the old man, "What's your name?"

The old man grumbled something and turned away.

Recognizing that the old man was in no mood to chat, Sam continued toward the window and up the stairs to the third floor.

Once in his room, Sam climbed upon his top bunk. The fresh oxygen in his brain brought a boatload of thoughts with it. *I wonder if those medals were his. I wonder how he got them. I wonder if he lives there. I wonder if he's mean enough to throw me off the roof....* Sam thought, his heart still pounding.

Sam glanced toward the roof. The old man had taken a seat in the tattered chair and pulled his hat down over his eyes as if planning on a long, restful nap. Jessie, as Sam would later learn his name to be, wasn't napping at all. He was thinking about this new intruder. *Is he the boy I've seen watching me from the window? What was he after? Did he say he hadn't been here before? It must be him.* And, secretly, he hoped his intruder would return so he could find out more about him.

The day after Sam's "visit" with the old man, Sam noticed him on the roof. Several of the birds were flying around him and the old man was smiling as if he were remembering days gone by. Sam leaned out his window just as the man looked in his direction. Sam waved and slowly the old man tipped his tattered hat.

After watching the old man that day, Sam decided that any man who danced and sang with pigeons couldn't be mean enough to hurt him. He knew that his first exploration of the roof was not going to be his last! He had to learn more about this mysterious old man, his medals, and his birds.

Chapter 5: It Has to Start Somewhere

One day after gym, Sam overheard Noah talking with some boys in the locker room about the old man and his pigeons. They were plotting to return to the roof to wreck the shack and hurt any birds they could find. There was still some fallout from the spaghetti episode so Sam slipped out the locker room door trying desperately not be seen. Sam knew he needed to warn the old man about Noah and his gang as quickly as he could

Later that same day, Sam mustered enough courage to head down to the second-floor window to tell the old man what he had heard. He didn't know what to expect after his last visit.

On the way, he ran into his grandmother who was on her way to help his mom bake cookies for an office party. Smokey, her small grey, wire-haired mixed terrier mutt, was trotting along behind her. Sam exchanged some greetings with his grandmother and gave her a hug. He also dutifully bent down to pet Smokey. After they parted, Sam thought, *Good. Gram will keep my mom distracted while I visit with the old man.* This was important because Sam's mom still had not given her permission for him to go to the roof.

Based on their last encounter, Sam cautiously climbed out the second-floor window. The height of the roof did not seem as intimidating this time though. He made his way carefully to the corner and stuck his head around. From there, he yelled, "PERMISSION TO COME ABOARD" and then he waited for the old man's reply. *What will I do if he doesn't respond?* thought Sam.

With his head poking around the corner, Sam could see the old man walking toward him. He stepped back from the corner, not wanting to appear too intrusive. *I should run now!* Sam thought. Instead, he held fast as the old man got closer to him. When the old man approached, Sam noticed a friendlier expression on his face as they exchanged greetings. Sam was relieved.

"The name's Jessie," blurted the old man. "And I believe you said your name was Samuel. Right?"

"Right, but my friends call me Sam. I need to tell you something important."

"Does your mother or father know you're here?" asked Jessie.

"Well, sort of...," Sam replied, feeling guilty for not telling the whole truth.

"Well, sort of isn't the right answer, Samuel. Bring one of your parents to the window to meet me. Then you can come aboard."

"I'll be back!" And with that, Sam headed back to the apartment to ask his mother to come to the second-floor window to meet Jessie.

His mom and grandmother had just started preparing for the baking when Sam entered the kitchen. Their aprons were on and their ingredients were on the porcelain-top table that sat in the middle of the kitchen.

"Mom, I need you to come with me!" Sam pleaded.

"Sam, can't you see we're in the middle of something?"

"This is important! You need to see. He is the man you know. His name is Jessie!"

"You mean the old man on the roof?"

"Yes. He said I couldn't come to the roof unless you give your permission. You have to come!"

"Well, I haven't given you my permission yet, young man!" But the fact that Jessie had told Sam to get his parent's permission immediately gave Sam's mom a good impression of him.

"I need more information for my book report," Sam responded hoping that would make it okay.

"I see. I guess I had forgotten about getting back to you," his mom replied.

Sam's grandmother reassured his mom that it would be a good thing to do and suggested, "You can go on down, Gayle. I'll get started with the baking while you are gone."

When Sam and his mom arrived at the window, Sam opened it.

"Hold on, young man! No one said anything about you stepping one foot on the roof!"

"No, I just want to yell for him," Sam explained and then waited for his mom's response.

She gave Sam an affirmative nod, so he opened the window and yelled for Jessie. It didn't take long for Jessie to come around the corner and approach the window. He removed his hat and respectfully said, "Howdy Ma'am."

"It is you, Mr. Walters! It is so good to see you! You were the maintenance man at my elementary school! It's me, Gayle, Gayle Jeffries. Well, at that time my last name was Abbott. I grew up right over there on Main Street; and my mom Sybil Abbott still lives there. It's so good to see you! It appears my son has way too much curiosity about your birds."

"Well, I'll be!" Jessie replied. "I can't say that I remember you; there were a lot of kids in that school. What would that have been—about 10 or 15 years ago?"

"Let's see. It would have been more like 20 or 25! Wow, time flies, doesn't it?" Gayle said to Jessie.

Jessie was quick with a reply, "It is very good to meet you again. You can call me Jessie. Would you like to check out the roof?"

"I'm not sure that it is safe for either of us to be on the roof, Jessie," said Gayle.

"Gayle, I think it's safe enough or I would not have encouraged it. I've been coming to this rooftop a long time. If Samuel is careful and responsible, he should not have any problems. Then Jessie directed his attention toward Sam, "That means staying away from the edge of the roof. Do you think you can do that, Samuel?" asked Jessie.

"Oh, yes sir, I can! Mom, can I go? Can I?"

"Not till I do," said Gayle. Even though she had gotten the reassurance from Jessie, she still had to check it out to make sure it was safe for an eleven-year-old boy to be on the roof and with Jessie. So, she managed to climb out the window with Jessie's assistance.

Once she was through the window and standing on the roof, she looked back at Sam. "This *is* very high, but I think there is plenty of room to get around safely without getting too close to the edge. I really like the barrier wall that goes around the roof!" It was about three and a half feet high, and the narrow walkway that led to the open roof was at least four or five feet wide.

"Just stay close to the wall, Gayle, and you will be fine." Jessie even offered to hold her hand as if she was still ten years old and he was still the maintenance man at Park Elementary. So, hand in hand, they proceeded around the corner, leaving Sam at the window fidgeting with excitement as most 11 year-old-boys would.

Before turning the corner to the open roof, Gayle turned back to Sam, "Stay there till I get back!" she said with a commanding tone.

Jessie showed Gayle around the campsite; they even went into the shack. In the shack, they talked about his years in the Air Force, his injury, and his Purple Heart. Gayle was impressed. They also talked about his Native American artwork. Jessie seemed proud to tell Gayle all about his Shawnee ancestry.

Obediently, Sam stood at the window, but on the inside his heart was racing with anticipation. He paced away from the window and then back at least ten times.

Meanwhile, Jessie and Sam's mom continued their tour. When they got to the bird cages, she turned to Jessie to say, "Wow, Jessie, the rooftop feels like a big open room. I can see why you like it."

"It's here I feel closest to the Great Creator, Gayle. Being on the rooftop helps me stay in touch with my roots. It's easier to keep my focus on the right things."

While they were on the roof, they also spent some time catching up on where life had taken them since they last saw each other. Gayle confided in Jessie that she had married Samuel Elliott Jeffries when she was a senior and that he had shipped out to Vietnam right after Jenna, their first child, was born. And then she concluded in a more somber tone, "He didn't come home from the war."

Jessie could see it was a difficult memory for her, and he didn't pry with any more questions. He did say, "Gayle, I'm sorry to hear that. I hope I can help Sam as his father would have."

"Thank you, Jessie. I think he needs that. Sam seems so angry most of the time," she said with a pause as she fiddled with the watch on her arm. Then she quickly added, "Do you live here?"

"No. I left Park Elementary after my wife died. I got depressed and used more alcohol than I should have. That's when I started coming to the roof — for healing. I may have drunk too much, but I wasn't stupid, Gayle! I knew I needed to keep my apartment on Holman Avenue for winter months. It's funny, though; most people think I'm homeless."

"I guess that would be an honest conclusion by folks if all they see is your being here. Are you still drinking?" Gayle asked with some degree of hesitancy.

"Oh, no, my dear! Getting back to my Native American roots has helped me put all that behind me."

"I'm glad for you," Gayle replied. After a few more minutes of chatting, Gayle told Jessie she had to get back to her cooking. But, before she left, she told him she was glad Sam wanted to hang out with him. They ended their conversation with a laugh and a hug.

The eight minutes they were gone seemed more like an hour to Sam; but when they did return, Sam's mom seemed much more comfortable about being on the roof and with Jessie. They were laughing about something that happened a long time ago as they came around the corner.

"Finally!" Sam exclaimed when he saw them come around the corner.

Gayle wanted to help Sam out the window, but he was so anxious to get there that he hopped through the window with ease. Little did Gayle know that Sam had managed quite well by himself once before when he went exploring through the portal. After a few final instructions, she crawled back through the window, leaving Sam in Jessie's care.

Once Sam and Jessie were near the shack, Jessie motioned for Sam to have a seat in the chair; and he grabbed another one from inside the shack. After Jessie was comfortably seated, they began their chat about a little bit of everything, but mostly pigeons!

"So, your name is Samuel?" Sam nodded. "Then, what was that "Sab" all about?"

He remembered that, thought Sam. That's when Sam went into the whole story about how he got his nickname. "But you can call me Sam," he quickly tagged onto the story.

After Gayle got back to the apartment, she went first to a window to see what was happening on the roof; and she returned to the window many times over the next hour and a half to make sure Sam was safe. She told her mom it was Jessie, the maintenance man, from her elementary school. And then she went on and on about how all the kids loved his stories about his military service and his Native American heritage. "I think Sabbie is safe with him," she concluded.

Gayle's mother, still in apron, looked up from what she was doing. She brushed her hair off her face, leaving a smudge of flour on her forehead. "Well, isn't that a coincidence?" she said. "That's good. Maybe a new adventure is just what Sam needs; and, Jessie can even be a man that Sam can look up to and learn from."

Meanwhile, back on the rooftop, Jessie and Sam continued their conversation. "Well, Sam, what is the important thing you need to tell me?"

"I heard those boys that were here in the summer talking about coming back to hurt your birds," said Sam.

"Well, thanks for the info, but they don't worry me too much. They are just into mischief. I just want them to leave us alone. Now, why are you so curious about this rooftop?" Jessie asked.

Thank goodness! Sam thought. *A way for me to get answers!* "May I call you Jessie?"

"Of course, unless you'd prefer to call me Chief?" said Jessie with a chuckle.

Hmmm, Sam thought. *Does that mean he is a Native American? I wonder if I could ask him.* He decided not; but, instead, he said, "Well, Jessie, I am writing a book report about pigeons and I wanted to hear what you had to say about them since you have a flock of them and all."

Jessie simply replied, "Okay. I like to talk about my birds."

Then Sam went on, "Also, there's this bird, see, and it comes to my window and wakes me up every morning. I think it is a pigeon and I wonder if it is one of yours."

"My birds are pigeons, but there are several types of pigeons. I'm not sure about the one that comes to your window."

Sam quickly blurted out, "Are you a squab farmer?" Since he had gotten squeamish in the library when he read about the tasty flesh of young pigeons, there was a bit of "YUK" in his tone of voice. With a smile on his face, Jessie reassured Sam that he most definitely was NOT a squab farmer.

That day Sam realized that Jessie did indeed like to talk about pigeons because before he could get out another word, Jessie began to talk about his birds. And then he talked, and talked, and talked.

"There are over 300 species of pigeons, each with their own unique markings and colors. One variety, the passenger pigeon, is now extinct. Martha, the last passenger pigeon on Earth, died in the Cincinnati Zoo in 1914.[11] One day we'll talk about why they became extinct.

"There are also rock pigeons. They're the kind you see around the city, cooing from the tops of buildings or in the park scratching for food.

"And there is a selectively bred variety of the rock pigeon called homing pigeons. They have the innate ability to carry messages long distances and still find their way back home."

Sam butted in, "I read about that in the book I got from the library!"

"I bet you've heard about G.I. Joe, haven't you?"

"Who hasn't heard of him?" said Sam shaking his head yes.

"Well, there was a homing pigeon named that too. He carried messages for Great Britain to the battlefields of WW II and later received the Dickin Medal of Honor[12] in 1946 for his service.[13] That's like the Purple Heart."

"Wow!" exclaimed Sam and then quickly tried to ask another question; but before he could, Jessie just kept going.

"And they are fast! Velocity was the name of a pigeon in Mr. Howie's Pigeon Post Service in New Zealand way back in 1896.[14] That bird could fly between Auckland and the Great Barrier Island in 50 minutes, almost as fast as any aircraft of that time!"

Then Jessie headed for the cages and Sam was right on his heels. Jessie reached in one of the cages and pulled out that favorite pigeon. She had markings that were somewhat different from the rest of the birds.

"Some of my birds are rock pigeons and some are homing pigeons. But this one is a special homing pigeon. She can fly low and slow or high and fast. That's why I call her B-52 after the Boeing B-52 Stratofortress, a military plane used for bombing!"

Sam couldn't contain himself! "That's the pigeon that has been coming to my window! I know it is!"

"I don't doubt it, Sam. She's a special bird. When she was young, I decided to enter her in a few of the pigeon races out West, just to see what she could do. She won all that she entered! But as we both got older, it just became too hard for me to travel around to the races so I stopped going to them. While she was racing, though, she got quite a name for herself."

"How old is she now, Jessie."

"She's thirteen years old," he replied.

"How long will she live?"

"Pigeons live about fifteen years. Those in captivity can live longer — into their late teens and early twenties," replied Jessie.[15]

"Gosh, then B-52 is old!" Sam remarked. He paused a bit but then went on with his questions. "How did you get them all? When did you get them? Do you use B-52 for any secret missions? Did you fly a B-52 Stratofortress? How do they know how to get home?"

"Wow, you have lots of questions, Sam," replied Jessie. We're going to need to answer some of those on a different day."

"Can I come back to see you then?" asked Sam.

"Of course, I look forward to it."

Sam scampered off the roof and back to the third floor. As soon as he entered the door, his mom and grandmother hurried to greet him and to see how it went.

"Sam, what did you and Jessie do? Did you get what you needed for your book report?" asked his mom.

"Oh, Mom, you won't believe it! He knows so much about pigeons. He has a homing pigeon named B-52! I want to visit him again. Can I?"

"Did he invite you to come back?"

"Yeah, he said, 'anytime.'"

"Then, okay, you have my permission to go back," replied his mom.

Sam ran to the window to see what his new friend was doing. He must have been in the shack because Sam couldn't see him on the roof. He decided to jot down some notes about the pigeons Jessie told him about. He knew he needed the references for this new information so he decided he would soon go to the library to get them. To remind himself, though, he wrote:

- Volocity (check spelling) – Fast, carried mail

- GI Joe – Dicking Metal – like Purple Heart
- Martha – Cincy Zoo – DEAD! Last of her kind.

This first official visit marked the beginning of a most unusual adventure for a fifth grade-boy.

Chapter 6: Finding Home

A few days later when Sam was in his room putting away his clothes, he noticed Jessie on the roof. He hurriedly finished putting his laundry away, then ran to the kitchen to tell his mom he was going down to the roof to visit Jessie. "I need to get some more information from him about homing pigeons for my book report. It's due next week," he said as he waved the index cards in front of her to convince her of his need to go.

"Have you finished putting away your clean clothes?" his mom asked.

"Yes, and I won't be gone long. I just need to find out how pigeons know to find their way home."

After his mom agreed, Sam headed for the roof. When he got there, he found Jessie in the shack. He knocked on the door and politely called out Jessie's name. "Jessie, it's Sam. Do you have time to talk?"

Jessie opened the door; Sam was glad to see his smile. "Sure, Sam. It's good to see you again," said Jessie.

"My book report is due next Friday and I have some more questions."

"Okay," said Jessie, as he motioned Sam toward the chairs beside the shack. After they were seated, Jessie continued, "Well, ask away."

And Sam did just that with a stream of questions that made Jessie's head spin. Then, Sam dropped a bombshell, "Do you think B-52 could get a message to my dad?"

Jessie's brow got those deep lines again. He was puzzled by this last question. He remembered what Gayle had said about her husband not making it home from the war. He assumed he had been killed in action. *Does Sam not know his dad is dead? Or is he? Is he MIA – missing in action? Or, did he just not come back?* Now Jessie was confused as these questions came to his mind.

Then, Jessie said very cautiously, "Homing pigeons just can't carry notes to random places, Sam. Since we don't know where your dad is, there is no way to train B-52 to get to him. Did you find any information in the library about homing pigeons' ability to find their way home?" asked Jessie.

Sam remembered one of his notecards. Homing pigeons use low-frequency sound waves to mentally map a path back to their loft. "I read something about sound waves," said Sam, "and that pigeons use them to map their way."

"Yes, the Great Creator gave homing pigeons the natural ability to navigate, much like the Creator gave humans the ability to learn to read. But just like we must learn to read, pigeons must learn how to carry messages to specific places. Do you want to know how they are trained? It might be good for your book report."

"Yes," Sam responded enthusiastically as he pulled the crumpled index cards from his back pocket.

"The way it works for most pigeons is by first establishing the pigeon post—their home. That is where they spend most of their time and where they eat. This rooftop is the pigeon post for my pigeons." Jessie moved over to the cages. "The cages of homing pigeons have a trap door that allows the pigeon to enter but restricts their ability to exit at will. [16] The pigeon post is the place where they will always return.

"For example, let's say you have a friend in Cincinnati," explained Jessie.

"I do," butted in Sam. "His name is Jerome."

"Okay," Jessie continued. "Let's say you and Jerome need to communicate and the only way you have to do it is by way of the pigeons. Wait a minute. Give me one of your notecards and a pencil." Then Jessie drew two cages on the notecard to show Sam how to train the pigeons. "Pigeons are natural navigators, Sam," as he labelled one of the cages "Jerome's loft, #1." Then he drew a second cage and labelled it "Sam's loft #2". To train your pigeon to go back and forth, you will need to carry your pigeon to Jerome's Loft #1 and leave it there.

And Jerome will have to carry his pigeon to your Loft #2 and leave it there." That way the pigeons can use their natural ability to mentally mark their path back to their own loft. From that point on, you can send the pigeons back and forth carrying your notes."

Sam thought about how cool it would be to send a note to Jerome. He envisioned his bird flying over the Ohio River, down Race Street, and landing on Jerome's window sill. Sam's daydreaming was interrupted by Jessie's words, "I've told you B-52 is special, haven't I? She doesn't follow those rules. She can go between this loft and another loft she has over near my apartment," Jessie explained.

"She is amazing!" Sam said with a grin.

Then Jessie recognized this as an opportunity to teach Sam about his own ability to navigate. He said, "When I was in the service, Sam, I was a navigator; and I used lots of instruments on the airplane to help the pilots get our aircraft home. Maybe that's why I started housing homing pigeons. I was fascinated about their natural ability to do what it took me and lots of instruments to do on the aircraft.

"But as I've worked with the pigeons over the years, I've come to believe that humans have a similar kind of navigation ability. What do you think, Sam? Do you think you have something in common with B-52?" asked Jessie.

"I'm not sure I understand what you mean, but I do think it is totally cool B-52 can do it!" replied Sam.

"I think you have a natural ability to navigate, Sam, similar to the homing pigeon. I think we all have instruments built inside us to help us find our way out of sadness, anger, and other things that would keep us from being happy and successful. I call it 'finding our way back home — to a place of peace in our mind and heart.' It took me a while to find that out."

Jessie noticed Sam was thinking hard about what he was saying, and he was impressed. But he was also still thinking about Sam's question about sending a message to his dad, Jessie went into the shack and got a piece of paper and a pencil from the small table beside his cot. When he came back, he said to Sam in a more serious tone, "You wanted to send a message to your dad. If you could send a message to your dad, what would it say? Use this paper to write it," Jessie said as he handed Sam the note paper.

Sam looked puzzled but he took the paper anyway. Then he wrote, "Daddy, where are you? I could use your help."

After Sam finished writing, Jessie said, "I'm not going to ask you to read it. Just fold it up and put it in your pocket. When you get back upstairs, put it someplace safe. Then, let's wait to see if you get any answers. It might take a while."

Sam did as Jessie instructed and stuffed the note in his pocket. Then Sam popped another question, "Jessie, if you've lived here a long time, you must have known my dad. Did you?"

Jessie stalled a bit as he took off his hat and rubbed the top of his head. He was thinking about what to say to an eleven-year-old boy who was missing his dad.

"Yeah, Sam, I remember the community having a special ceremony for some high school boys who had enlisted in the Army during the Vietnam War. I think your dad was one of them."

Sam interrupted Jessie, "Then he <u>was</u> a soldier! Was he a hero? Killed in action? Did he win a medal like you have hanging on your wall?"

Jessie started to fidget a bit and suggested Sam have this conversation with his mother. "But she won't talk about it!" Sam said in a frustrated, almost tearful voice.

Jessie was puzzled about the secrecy around Sam's dad and decided to respond carefully, "Sam, I don't know what happened to your dad. I do know that your dad must have been a brave warrior to sign up for the Army during war time. You should be proud of him for that."

"I guess," replied Sam.

Jessie, being uncomfortable with this conversation, decided that the visit had gone on long enough. "I'm getting tired, Sam. Maybe we can meet again another day."

Sam headed for the window. His stooped shoulders and bowed head reflected his disappointment about his unanswered questions. Jessie could see his torment. And then he said, "Sam, wait! I want to give you something."

Sam turned toward Jessie who had gone into the shack. He emerged a few minutes later with a feathered object in his hand. "Sam, this is a friendship feather made with the feathers of a falcon. I'd like you to have it because I think we are going to be great friends."

Sam was very pleased and responded with a polite, "Thank you, Jessie."

Sam left the roof with the feather in his hand. He was happy to have met Jessie, his unusual friend; but he also felt angry. As he walked toward the second-floor window, his thoughts became ugly and mean — *Daddy, even stupid birds can find their way back home. Why can't you?*

When he got back to his bedroom, he tied the friendship feather on the post of his bed and touched its soft feathery edges. He then took the note he had written to his dad out of his pocket and read it again. *"Daddy, where are you? I could use your help."* Sam felt sad because he couldn't get the note to his dad, and he angrily stuffed it into his box of feathers.

Jessie, on the other hand, retreated to his shack and sat down on the cot. He wondered how he might help Gayle give Sam the answers he needed about his dad.

Chapter 7: Communications

By late November, the fallout from the hat incident was long gone; and to Sam, it was ancient history, especially since he had gotten an A+ on his book report. Sam was happy with the grade, but he was even happier to read the note his teacher wrote on the front page of his report. "Sam, great job! Your work reflects in-depth research and your personal experience with the topic. Keep up the good work! P.S. I loved the illustrations of the pigeon lofts!" For the first time, he felt like things were actually going right for him at school.

One day, he noticed Jessie putting things away on the rooftop. It looked like he was leaving it for the winter. *I wonder where he's going. I need to find out,* Sam thought as he hurried down to the roof.

"Hi Chief," Sam said as he came around the corner.

"Hello, young warrior," Jessie replied.

"What are you doing?"

"I can't stay here during the winter, Sam; you know that. But I'll be back next spring. I have an apartment over on Holman Avenue."

"Where will the pigeons go?" asked Sam.

"Pigeons don't fly south for the winter so I have a roost for them in a warehouse over on 12th Street. A friend lets me use it during winter months."

"You mean Loft #2?" asked Sam.

"Well kind of. It's their second loft, but I'm not sending any messages by them between lofts."

Once Sam knew that Jessie and the birds would be safe over the winter, he was satisfied knowing the rooftop would come alive again the following spring. "Well, I'll miss you and the birds," said Sam choking up just a bit.

"Oh, sprout, it will go quickly! You have the holidays to look forward to. I'll be back by next Easter," Jessie said as he headed into the shack to put away some things.

Sam followed Jessie into the shack. "Is there anything I can do to help you?"

"I don't think so, Sam. Maybe you could just keep an eye on the place while I am gone."

"Oh, I will," said Sam enthusiastically. As he watched Jessie work, Sam decided to apologize again for snooping before they met. Then, he started asking questions about the items he saw. He was especially interested in the wall hanging. "What is this, Jessie?" asked Sam.

"It is a dreamcatcher. My people, the Shawnee, believe that dreams are messages that come from the sacred spirits. Some tribes believe that the hole in the middle catches the good dreams to be passed on to the sleeper. The web traps all the bad dreams; and then at the first light of morning, the bad dreams disappear.

"The way a dreamcatcher is made is based on other beliefs within each tribe. As you can see, it has lots of feathers on it. And there is a reason for that.

"Do you remember I told you that feathers have special meaning to Indians? We use feathers to symbolize trust, honor, strength, wisdom, power, freedom, and many more things. To be given a feather is a high honor."

"I've been collecting some feathers when I see them," said Sam and then he asked his next big question. "Do you think they are messages from the 'other side?' I read about that in one of my library books." He thought he might not like to know the answer.

"Yes, I think they can be." Jessie responded.

Sam was in awe listening to Jessie talk about feathers and their importance within the Shawnee culture; but he interrupted by saying, "Most of my feathers are from B-52. What's the message there?"

"She brought you to the roof, didn't she?"

Sam liked the thought of that! And he wondered if he'd get other messages. "Speaking of messages, Jessie, I've seen you taking notes off B-52. Who are you sending notes to? Is it a secret mission?"

"Well, Sam, it is a secret—it's a very private thing!" as he started walking toward the second-floor window. Sam followed along saying he was sorry for intruding. And Jessie patted him on the shoulder and said, "That's okay. Just remember that it is important to respect others' privacy."

"I understand," said Sam as they said their good-byes.

Back in his room, Sam looked down at the rooftop. *I should not have said anything about those notes,* Sam thought. He was frustrated with himself for being so nosey.

As he scanned the rooftop, it made him sad to see it vacant. The chairs were stacked and covered with a heavy tarp. *I'll miss him and the birds,* thought Sam as he looked through his window.

But he didn't have to miss any of it long. The very next morning, it was there again! The nuisance at the window. "It's B-52!" Sam said in a loud whisper. Joey wiggled in his bed.

"It's okay, Joey. Go back to sleep," Sam said.

Then Sam quietly and very, very slowly opened the window. For the first time, B-52 did not fly away. Sam first stroked the top of her head. Then, he picked her up with his hands cupped beneath her as he had seen Jessie do so many times. "She has a note!" he said out loud. Joey rolled over again. Then Sam took the note from B-52's foot and read, "Warrior, the battle is near. Are you ready? Jessie."

Sam wondered what he meant, but he decided to play along with the game. Quickly, he scribbled a note, "Chief, bring it on! Sam." He then attached it to the foot of B-52 and off she went.

Well into winter, Sam and Jessie sent notes back and forth on the foot of B-52 about the need to prepare for this fictitious battle — what Sam would need and what he should be prepared to do. Sometimes, though, the notes were just the usual "Hi, how are you?"

Then the notes became focused on Sam completing some real secret missions focused on doing nice things for others. One time, Jessie asked Sam to do something nice for a teacher at school. Sam decided to make his math teacher a 'thank you' card for all her extra effort helping him with his math. Jessie always wanted to know what he did and how the mission turned out. "Well, what did you do? And, what was the outcome?" was the note on B-52's foot.

Sam was proud to return B-52 with his note about the teacher secret mission, "When she opened it, she smiled at me. I liked doing it."

When Spring came, Sam realized the importance of these notes for communicating with his unique friend.

Chapter 8: Broken Spirits

Even though Sam thought the "hat escapade" was over, that didn't turn out to be true. Noah wouldn't let it go. He had begun to put actions to his snarly looks and words. One day, he had even put some of the spaghetti he had at lunch in Sam's book bag. Mostly, though, he liked to prove his dominance over others; and Sam was one of his favorite targets. When he cornered Sam in the locker room, he was careful not to leave any cuts or bruises on Sam's face or neck.

Sometimes Noah was alone, and sometimes he brought a couple of other guys with him. Like most times, he wanted something from Sam—any money he had, his science homework, a new gym bag. But mostly, Noah just wanted to prove to Sam that he could take what he wanted from him or remind him about the spaghetti fight. And Sam let him.

Shortly after Easter break, Noah learned of Sam's infatuation with Jessie and the pigeons. After that, he was determined to shame or hurt Sam even more. And, he acted on his words one day when he saw Sam alone in the park feeding some pigeons.

"Dude, why are you in our park?" threatened Noah.

"I didn't realize you owned it," responded Sam in a snarky tone.

"So, you want to be funny, huh?" said Noah and bent over in a hearty laugh that was as fake as his declared ownership of the park. When he raised up, he took a swing at Sam, hitting him square in the belly. Sam fell backward and landed on the concrete sidewalk. "Well, this is our turf, and you need to stay out of it!" gloated Noah as he stood over Sam. "What're ya gonna do now, Sabbie?" Noah taunted in a deliberate whiny tone that drew out and emphasized Sam's nickname.

Sam stayed down for a bit but then struggled to get up. That's when he felt the blood pushing through the veins in his neck and down his arms and finally into his legs. Before he could even think about it, he just took a giant dive into Noah, grabbing him around the waist and pulling him to the ground. After rolling around on the ground, they both realized they had rolled into a bicycle. And then they saw feet. They had rolled into Officer Epstein who was on patrol in the park.

After a brief lecture from the police officer about fighting, they parted; but as they were leaving, Noah whispered to Sam, "This ain't over, punk!"

This was one of those times when Sam needed his dad — another man to turn to for advice on how to fight a bully. He thought he might get Troy's advice, but he was a senior in high school. He would be graduating soon, and he didn't seem to have much time for Sam any more.

So, he waited for Jessie to come back, but to no avail. Finally, B-52 showed up and Sam was ready. He had scribbled a note to Jessie, "Chief, the battle is upon us! Come back! Sam." He attached the note and off B-52 went.

Like clockwork, she returned the following morning with a note on her leg. Sam recognized the paper immediately. It was the same paper he had seen lying on the table in the shack. It said, "I'm coming to the roof tomorrow. Jessie."

When Sam got home from school the following day, he was excited to find Jessie on the roof. He couldn't wait to see him and talk to him about Noah and his bully friends.

He found Jessie by the pigeon cages.

"Hi Jessie. How are you? Thanks for coming so soon. That note thing is very cool!"

"I thought you'd like the notes. So, what's this about the 'battle upon us,' Sam?" asked Jessie.

And then Sam began to tell Jessie about Noah. "I'm having some trouble with those boys who were on the roof chasing the pigeons. They make me so mad!"

"I heard!" said Jessie.

"From who?" asked Sam.

"Do you mean from whom?"

"I don't know, do I?"

"Don't be a smart aleck, Sam! You know what I mean. To answer your question, I still have friends over at the elementary school, and word gets around. So, you threw some spaghetti, did you?" asked Jessie.

"Yeah, and he's never let me forget it," said Sam. "Earlier this week, we got into a fight in the park. Officer Epstein stopped it or I probably would have been hurt. Noah is older and much bigger than I am."

Jessie did not like hearing about Sam's trouble with the bullies. Since Sam seemed to be looking for some fatherly advice, Jessie decided to use Sam's nickname; and Sam didn't mind it at all when Jessie used it.

Jessie started out, "Sab, we have to find a way for you to stand up to those boys once and for all! A long time ago, I had my share of bullies too," Jessie said. "Do you think it was easy being the only Indian in my fifth-grade class?"

"I guess not."

"The first time I was bullied was during the Great Depression[17]. I was about your age. During that time, most families across the country suffered financially."

Oh, my goodness, Sam thought, *what on earth does that have to do with Noah and this bruise on my back?* But respectfully, Sam listened.

Jessie continued, "People were out of jobs. It seemed like everyone was poor. Children were expected to help make money for the family. My job was to collect returnable, glass bottles by rummaging through garbage cans, along alleys, and in yards. The six-ounce, returnable coca cola bottles would bring three cents at the store; some bottles brought more.

"My mother expected me to bring home at least forty or fifty cents a day so my day started early. She would hand me a biscuit and jelly for breakfast and a large burlap bag for my bottles and send me on my way. So, like most twelve-year-old boys, I did what I was told."

Good grief, get to the point, Jessie! Sam thought.

On Jessie droned, "I had the same routine for finding 15-20 bottles every day. On a good bottle-finding day, I would treat myself to some peanuts and a cold soda on the steps of McIntyre's Market on 4th Street — basically costing about four coke bottles."

At this point, Sam wanted to roll his eyes, but he managed to stifle his impatience a bit longer.

"As you might suspect, I got called a few names for running around with a burlap sack over my shoulder," Jessie continued.

Finally, some focus, Sam thought.

"One of the names that stuck was Bottleneck." Sam's ears perked up and he leaned closer toward Jessie.

"Once, I was passing the park with my bag nearly full of bottles when I saw some boys playing basketball. I stopped and wished I could join in. Instead, they heard the clanking of my bottles and the situation got tense. One of them said, 'Hey, Bottleneck, did you find enough bottles for your momma today?' I just kept walking, trying to ignore them but they wanted to 'play' — and not basketball!

"One of them jumped right in front of me. 'I'm talkin' to you bottle boy,' the bigger boy said and pushed me backwards over the back of another boy who had crept up behind me and knelt down. I hit the cement along with the sack of bottles. The sound of breaking glass hurt my head almost as much as the concrete. As I was trying to get up, another boy grabbed my bag and tossed it high in the air, letting it crash to the ground. I seriously wanted to cry or lash out at them — I didn't know which.

"I had so many emotions running through me that I could do nothing. I just lay there. Then, Mrs. Edwards, whose husband ran the dry-cleaning store on the edge of the park, appeared wielding a broom in one hand and yelling for the kids to stop. They scattered like a flock of pigeons when startled — all but me. I just lay there. She came over to me to see if I was okay and to help me up. Together, we cleaned up the shards of glass from the playground.

"She could see how embarrassed I was as I sheepishly said 'thank you' and she tried to make light of it. But like most kids who get bullied, I felt ashamed and weak. Later, I looked through my damaged bag and found only two bottles that remained unbroken."

Then, staring down at his wrinkled hands, Jessie paused for quite some time. The silence was thick like a heavy smoke that tightens your chest. Sam waited. He moved his chair closer anticipating important words of wisdom.

"You know, Sam, about five years after that incident happened, I was sitting on the front steps with a few of my friends. Mrs. Edwards came shuffling down the street with a little wagon behind her. The wagon was filled with canned goods and other items from the grocery. A man running down the street bumped into her causing her wagon to tip over. The man just kept running, and some of the cans came rolling over right in front of the stoop where my friends and I were sitting."

"What did you do, Jessie? asked Sam.

"Sam, I was 17 and too embarrassed to let my friends see me helping an old lady pick up her things. I didn't do anything like all my friends. We just let her pick up her stuff and head on down the street. Not helping her out after she had helped me is something that I am not proud of!"

Sam shuffled in his chair at this awkward moment. He could see Jessie's embarrassment. "But then you joined the Air Force, didn't you?" Sam said wanting to praise Jessie for his bravery.

"Yeah, I did; but it would have been just as brave to get up off my butt and help Mrs. Edwards who had helped me." And then Jessie went on. "After I joined the Air Force, they sent me to Jefferson Barracks. In the Commissary, I picked up a book that had a quote in it from Winston Churchill. He said that 'courage is rightly esteemed the first of human qualities… because it is the quality which guarantees all the others.'[18] What do you think that means, Sam?"

Sam thought for a minute and then said, "Who is Winston Churchill?"

Jessie smiled and then told Sam that Churchill was a soldier and a statesman. He served as the Prime Minister of Britain twice. One of those times was during WWII. And then he concluded, "So what do you think he meant when he said, 'It is the quality that guarantees all the others?'"

"I guess it means it takes courage to live," replied Sam.

"You are a smart boy, Sam. That's exactly what it means. Performing a simple act of kindness like picking up Mrs. Edwards' groceries takes courage. Going to school every day takes courage. Serving the military takes courage. And, standing up to Noah takes courage."

"I don't feel courageous at all," Sam said. "When I see him, I want to run away and hide."

"You have courage already within you. It's been growing with you. Do you know how I know that?" asked Jessie.

"How?"

"It took courage for you to come through that window over there last summer and meet a strange old man. And it took courage for you to come here today to talk to me about Noah."

"Well, last summer, I was just curious about the birds," said Sam.

"It started with curiosity, but it took courage to pursue it. Our courage emerges with each challenge we face. It's a combination of chemicals in our body that helps us to survive and the sheer will or determination to live. We must want it.

"Now let's figure out what to do with Noah and his friends. Do you know what it means to be cunning?"

"I've heard 'cunning like a fox.' I think it means being sneaky."

"That's about it. It's using your wits to survive. Trickery might be part of it. You must find your own way for dealing with Noah because you might have this challenge with other bullies at different times in your life. Bullying is not just a kid thing."

Wits? Sam thought, but he just responded politely, "But, I don't know how!"

"Let your head guide you and not your emotion. You are already using your wits! You are doing the most important thing about a bully at school. You are talking to someone you trust. I'm glad you are talking to me but don't be afraid to tell your mom or someone you trust at school where they can help you more than I can. You don't have to be alone in this."

Sam told Jessie he appreciated his help and then their conversation turned to pigeons and other fun things. On his way back to his room, Sam thought again about their conversations and his problem with Noah. *How am I — a kid — supposed to know how to handle stuff like this?*

Chapter 9: The Falcon's Feast

Sam came home to quite a surprise one day in the spring. He took one look in his bedroom and shouted, "Joey, what have you done? Mom, Mom, look what Joey has done!" His mother came running into the room. On the desk was a piece of artwork that Joey had created with glue, coloring pencils, and feathers. She saw feathers scattered on his bed and the floor. Then her eyes found the overturned box labelled "Hands Off! This is Sam's." She closed her eyes and took a deep breath. *This is not going to be easy*, she thought.

"Mom, I made you this picture," said Joey proudly.

She didn't know what to say to Joey or Sam. She could see both their faces with quite different expressions. It was hard for Sam's mom to raise three kids by herself. This was one of those times when she wished she had some help to respond to Joey who was so needy and so proud of his artwork. She knew she had to praise Joey for his kindness; but at the same time, she had to teach him to respect his brother's things.

And she also had to console Sam about his brother's intrusion and loss of his prized collection. She tried as best she could to meet the challenge; but in the end, she only felt sad and bewildered about the way she had handled it. She ended up posting Joey's artwork on the refrigerator and tolerating Sam storming out of the apartment in a huff.

Sam went directly to the roof to check on the birds. After their conversation in the spring about bullies, Jessie had stopped coming to the roof regularly as he had done in the past, and B-52's notes had stopped too.

Sam had wondered where Jessie was because the birds were still coming to the roost. And, because Jessie wasn't there, Sam also wondered if he should be caring for the birds. After a couple of weeks had passed, Sam became even more worried that something might have happened to Jessie.

When Sam got to the roof, he decided it was a good time to look around for clues about Jessie's absence. In the shack, most everything was still there. When he saw the sack of bird seed in the corner, he was reminded of his task. He filled the birds' feeding trays as Jessie had taught him.

For two weeks, Sam took the job of feeding the birds responsibly. Since Jessie still had not returned, Sam even tried to follow the practice of sending them off in the morning and greeting them back to the roost at night. Finally, his concern about Jessie convinced him it was time to send another note to Jessie on B-52's foot.

He took a piece of paper from the small table in the shack and on it he wrote: "Jessie, where are you? The pigeons need you!" And he sent B-52 off one morning. She came back that evening on schedule with a note on her leg. Sam was eager to retrieve it. It said, "Jessie, where are you? The pigeons need you!"

"What?" yelled Sam. "This is the same note!" Frustrated, he quickly put B-52 in her cage. *Stupid pigeon!* he thought as he closed the door. That was the last note Sam sent for a while.

After Sam had turned eleven on his last birthday in November, he enjoyed more freedom in the neighborhood by spring. Even though he could go to the park and a few other places by himself, he preferred being on the roof even without sending messages. But he also thought it would be more fun to get a couple of his friends to join him. Of course, he thought of his two best friends, Dave and Alex. He decided he wouldn't say anything about notes to them.

Dave had told Sam all about his foster family and that this was his third placement. There were two more boys who lived in the same foster home — his "foster brothers," Dave said. One of the boys was black and one was a mixed race. "My foster family looks like a strange lot, but it's all good," he concluded. "It's better than the last two!"

Dave kind of brought Alex into the picture not long after the hat incident. After that day, all the kids were talking about the "new kid" who threw spaghetti in Noah's face. Sam had not been the only kid to get bullied by Noah, so anyone who stood up to him would be something of a hero. Alex told Dave how cool he thought Sam was. That's when Dave invited Alex to join him for a game or two of basketball with Sam. They hit it off right away. They all seemed to like the same things so the three boys became best friends for the remainder of their elementary school years.

"Dave is quiet, respectful, and responsible. I like him a lot," Sam's mom once told him. "He's level-headed, and I trust that when you are with him, you are less likely to do silly things."

Boy, does Dave have her fooled! Sam thought.

Yes, Dave was quite the opposite. It was Dave who liked to push the limits of anything they were doing. He was quick witted and could make the boys laugh about almost anything so the boys had lots of fun together. But, it was also Dave who got Sam and Alex into some uncomfortable predicaments at times.

For example, during the summer Dave encouraged them to have a campout on the roof. They all agreed and decided to bring different things. Sam raided the kitchen for some snacks. He came up with peanut butter and jelly sandwiches and some fruit juice, a half-full bag of chips, and two apples. Dave and Alex brought some other snacks. They were eager to see what it was like to sleep under the stars.

Turns out, there were other things besides pigeons that flew around on the roof — bats to be specific! Sam and his friends made makeshift helmets to protect their heads from the bats, but it wasn't long before Alex decided that sleeping in the shack would be a better idea. They flipped a coin for who could have the cot to sleep on, and Sam won the toss. Dave and Alex made a pallet out of blankets on the floor.

Into the night, Sam heard a different kind of commotion outside the shack. He listened a while and then roused his friend Dave. "There's someone outside," Sam whispered. "What are we going to do?"

"Maybe it's Jessie," replied Dave half asleep.

Without knowing for sure, Sam told Dave to be perfectly still. And he did — right down to his breathing. Sam and Dave peeked through the boards of the shack to see if they could tell who was on the roof. Sam felt Dave's body shrink in size when they saw two men pilfering around the knapsacks they had left outside. Then, they heard the intruders moving closer to the shack.

Dave scampered back under the blanket on the floor with Alex; Sam stood near the door. The men were by the bird cages, and the birds were fluttering and squawking. They heard one man say, "Put it in the box. It might be the one."

"They're taking one of the pigeons!" Sam whispered urgently to Dave. Dave was too afraid to reply.

When the thieves came to the shack door, the boys' hearts nearly stopped. Just as the door started to open, someone in one of the apartments on the third floor flipped on a light and it must have startled the thieves. They stopped and whispered something to each other that the boys couldn't understand.

When the light went back off, the thieves opened the door. That's when they saw Sam's shadowy figure standing near the opening. The thieves had not yet seen Alex and Dave, still cowering beneath the blanket on the floor. Sam tried to remember Jessie's words about courage. He knew he was going to need some. "It's something that wells up inside you when you feel threatened. It's a combination of chemicals in your body and the will to survive," Jessie had said.

Well, I hope it's working, Sam thought!

One of the thieves bellowed, "Where's the old man?" Alex actually squealed.

"Shhhhh," whispered Dave.

Then the thief who was standing in the door pointed the flashlight beam right in Sam's face and demanded, "Where is the old man? We want that bird."

Stepping back from the door and tripping over Dave's leg, Sam tried courageously to reply, "He's not here. He hasn't been here in a long time. We don't know anything about where he went."

When a dog started barking in one of the apartments overlooking the roof, the thieves just turned and hurriedly left the roof with one of the pigeons squawking in a box.

As soon as he heard the men leave, Sam whispered to the boys, "You can come out now. Let's get out of here!" And they retreated to Sam's bedroom, each with their own tale about thieves.

Once safely in his room, Sam wondered why the men would want to steal Jessie's pigeons and which *one* they were interested in? He decided he needed to get more information about squab farming to see if it could be related to what happened.

The next morning following breakfast, Sam, Dave, and Alex decided to go check out the roof to see if the thieves had come back. By the time they got there, the pigeons had all left their roost. That's when Alex and Dave went home and Sam went to the library. This time he went straight to the card catalogue to find books on squab farming. To his surprise, he found several different books and carried them to a table for further reading.

He saw lots of pictures, found lots of facts, and learned more about how homing pigeons were used in WWII, just as Jessie had described. One book titled *A to Z of Pigeons, Fancy and Utility* was what he was looking for.

It was an eye opener all right! In the section on utility pigeons, Sam read about the farms specifically designed to raise young, specially-bred pigeons for their meat. As he read more, he thought, *Could this be connected to the men wanting Jessie's pigeons?*

Sam learned that squab, or young pigeon, had been bred as food for centuries — even as far back as the medieval times. It was considered a delicacy for kings, emperors, and pharaohs. As Sam read more about the dark, moist, flavorful taste of four-week-old hatchlings, he felt his breakfast begin to climb out of his stomach and into his throat. He gagged a bit. *Oh, please don't let them be squab farmers after the pigeons and especially not B-52!* Sam thought. He left determined to inform Jessie all about the thieves and their intent. *Jessie, please come back,* he thought as he was leaving the library. *I need to talk to you!*

Desperate to reach Jessie, Sam decided to send another note on B-52's leg the very next morning. "Jessie, thieves want the birds. Come back. Sam." He sent her off early in the day; and in the evening, he went to the roof to wait for her to return. Thankfully, she came back on schedule, and there was a note on her leg. It read, "Don't let them hurt the birds! I'll be back in a few weeks."

Sam was so excited his note had reached Jessie that he yelled out loud, "Jessie got it!" And from then on, he took the job of feeding and protecting the birds very seriously as Jessie had requested.

Within a week, Sam and his friends had forgotten about the thieves; and they resumed their frequent visits to the roof. Besides, all three boys thought their summer was way too boring without their rooftop hangout.

Eventually, the boys decided to make the rooftop look more like their hangout. Dave brought a can of white spray paint to make a sign and some not-so-nice artwork that Sam wouldn't let him hang anywhere. Alex brought a couple of old lawn chairs.

Sam was adamant about keeping things on the inside intact. "Jessie will be back," Sam insisted.

There were some boards stacked up near the shack that the boys used to make a makeshift backboard for a basketball rim. The boards must have been left over from when Jessie built the shack because they were the same wood. Dave confiscated one of the boards and painted "Friends Forever" on it. They hung their goal and net on the side of the shack.

Not two days later, Jessie returned and none too soon for Sam! Yep, one day when the boys were trying to shoot hoops using the rickety makeshift backboard, Jessie came hobbling around the corner on a pair of crutches. His eyes quickly scanned the scene in front of him but landed on the makeshift basketball backboard and hoop.

Sam, feeling a bit embarrassed in this awkward situation, ran to Jessie and gave him a big hug. Jessie hugged back; but with it came a demanding question about their occupation of the roof—squatting, he called it.

"What's squatting?" Dave asked.

"It's all this!" replied Jessie. "You've taken over my territory!"

Jessie's reaction hit a nerve with Sam; and he remembered how he felt when Joey had intruded in his space, leaving only the trail of feathers behind. He realized what Jessie must be feeling.

Sam stammered around until he came up with a story about it being hot in his room—which was partly true! Then, an explanation rattled out of his mouth about feeding and protecting the pigeons. "There were thieves who came to get a pigeon—a specific one," Sam told Jessie.

___

76

"I got the note. Tell me more about the thieves," said Jessie.

Alex started an elaborate tale about the thieves, "They were snooping through our bags and looking in the cages. We were sleeping in the shack. They came to the door and nearly scared us to death! We think they even took one of the birds!"

Jessie walked over and sat in a chair. He didn't let on to the boys what he suspected the thieves were after. Sam later learned that Jessie had been contacted many times by commercial squab growers to enlist his help in finding the most select birds to populate their meat supply. Squab was in high demand, but Jessie had always turned them down. Jessie thought surely the farmers had decided to take matters into their own hands.

But Jessie was also curious about why they might want one specific bird. That made him think the thieves might be after B-52 for racing because of her success in Texas and California when she was younger.

After their brief discussion of bird thieves, Sam diverted the conversation away from their "squatting" with a question about Jessie's evident injury. It worked! Jessie started telling the boys the reason he had been gone for a while. They thought it was a story worth listening to.

Jessie told them he was in the Air Force, one of many paratroopers during WW II. There had been lots of training for the jumps into different terrain, war zones, etc. But every jump was different, Jessie explained. He and his troop made more than 100 jumps before the last one Jessie made with them in 1943.

Jessie's last jump was to land on a beach in France, along with five other guys. Their mission was a scouting expedition for a military advance to come later. As they got near the beach, the wind drifted his chute toward the jagged rocks that jutted from a cliff above the beach. He maneuvered the chute toward a stretch off to the right; but he hadn't been able to see the deep, narrow caverns between the boulders on the cliff. He landed, wedging his right leg up to the upper thigh in one of the caverns.

Realizing he was injured, the other jumpers on the beach below radioed for a medivac helicopter. It took four hours to free him. When he got to the army hospital, there was severe nerve damage in his leg.

After he left the military hospital, he was trained as a navigator to serve out his remaining years in the Air Force. After he had served six years, the pain was too great for him to continue. He was discharged honorably, with a disability check and almost constant pain to deal with the rest of his life. He told the boys that was why in April, when his pain worsened, he checked into the VA Hospital in Cincinnati for some trial procedures to block the constant, painful nerve impulses in his feet, legs, and back.

As Jessie shared his story, Sam and his friends sat quietly with mouths gaped and eyes opened wide. When Jessie finished, they hurriedly began to collect their things and put Jessie's things back the way they were. But Jessie stopped the boys from removing the extra chairs, the basketball hoop, and the "Friends Forever" sign. "I like your additions," he said. "You should leave them!" Afterwards, they all spent the rest of the afternoon together enjoying some snacks and listening to more of Jessie's stories.

After Jessie's visit, Sam and his friends enjoyed many more days and nights on the roof. Sam wanted to make sure the birds got enough to eat and were safe from the bird thieves. One night as the pigeons were coming home to roost, a falcon swooped down and grabbed one of the pigeons in mid-air — right in front of Sam's eyes! The falcon held the pigeon with its powerful claws and flew away. Shocked, Sam just stood there watching the mighty bird become nothing but a speck in the sky. Sam was so bewildered that he almost cried.

Sam was eager to tell Jessie about the falcon, but Jessie did not come to the roof very often. Jessie had told Sam that it was more difficult for him to climb out the window. What Jessie didn't tell Sam was that he also had some things to do about squab farmers and hooligans.

On the few occasions that Jessie did return, he and Sam would catch up on what was happening, as friends do. The first chance he got, Sam began telling Jessie about the falcon, "I'm sorry I couldn't protect them all. It was horrible to hear the pigeon squawking as the hawk disappeared into the blue sky."

Jessie saw the falcon's feast as an opportunity to talk to Sam about his dad. "Do you remember that your friendship feather is made with falcon feathers?"

"Yes, I have it hanging on my bed post," answered Sam.

"Do you know the symbolism of that feather?"

"No, you never told me that. I thought it meant friendship."

"Well, yes and no. The object did signify friendship; but the falcon feather is given to those who need healing — not in their body, but deeper inside — in their spirit. Maybe it wasn't a coincidence that the falcon approached you that day," said Jessie. "Do you think the falcon could have been trying to tell you something?"

"What do you mean?" Sam asked with his eyes so wide Jessie thought they might pop out of his head.

"The falcon got in your face—big time—wouldn't you say?"

"Yeah, I was so shocked! I had never seen anything like it."

"Sam, I know Noah is a challenge to you. He is harassing you, and you are afraid of getting hurt. But it seems like there is another challenge that is hiding in your heart, and it might be more harmful than Noah to you in the long run. And I think it relates to your dad."

"I know I miss not having a dad around."

"I understand that, young warrior. I think that desperate longing is causing you to miss out on the joy of your youth. Maybe the episode of the falcon's feast was telling you it's time for you to use your wisdom and courage to understand and heal that hole in your heart before it gets worse.

Sam was trying hard to listen but it was hard for such a young boy to understand some of the things Jessie was saying.

Jessie continued, "Challenges are like the falcon's mighty claws. If you don't resolve them, they might grab you around the throat and carry you off."

With eyes wide open, Sam just sat there visualizing being grabbed by the throat. He couldn't understand the depth of what Jessie was saying.

Before long, Jessie realized he was talking to himself— that Sam's attention had already left the roof. He told Sam it was time to call it a day. As they started toward the window, Sam noticed that Jessie was carrying a small sack with some of the things from the shack. He was puzzled about it, but he decided not to pry.

As they got to the window, Jessie turned to Sam to say, "Sam, you took the job of protecting the birds very seriously and I am proud of you. You should be proud of yourself, too."

Chapter 10: Out of Control

Near the end of summer as Sam was going into sixth grade, Joey shocked Sam so bad that he forgot about pigeons and falcons for quite some time. Sam was on the roof and looked up toward his bedroom. He saw Joey sitting in the window yelling something about B-52 and a feather. He had straddled the window sill with one leg hanging outside the window so Sam knew he had to get to him *fast!*

Sam ran so hard and so fast up the stairs that he even amazed himself. He prayed the entire way! "Please, God; oh please, God." When he got to his bedroom and took Joey out of the window, Joey was holding a white dove feather! Joey said proudly that he had found the feather on the window sill. "It's for your collection!" Joey said.

"Joey, you must never get in the window like that again. You can get hurt!"

"I'm sorry, Sabbie," Joey replied.

"That's okay; I just don't want you to get hurt," said Sam as he gave Joey a hug. "Thank you for the feather."

"Do you like it?" asked Joey.

"I do, Joey, but please promise me you won't get in the window again like that! Will you keep the feather for me?" asked Sam.

"I will, I will, I will keep Sabbie's feather for him," Joey sang as he scampered off down the hall.

Sam still sat stunned on Joey's bunk from the ordeal, and he realized that his obsession with the birds had almost caused Joey to be hurt or killed. He had not realized that his little brother was watching his antics on the roof with the birds, and he realized he needed to be a better big brother to him.

Sam did just that for the rest of July and the beginning of August. He tried to spend more time with Joey by taking him to the park and to the library for story time. They also visited the Mr. Softie ice-cream truck on more than one occasion when they had the money to buy the soft-serve ice cream. It was Joey's favorite.

During that same time, Sam's interest in basketball replaced some of his obsession with the birds. He, Dave, and Alex (the Three Musketeers, as they called themselves) started playing basketball in the school yard; and they needed five players. Brian and James were the ones that hung around the courts most often so they were added to make the five-person team. Over time, they all became good friends, and they now referred to themselves as "The Fearless Five."

Brian was tall and lanky. He had let his black hair grow past his ears till it brushed the top of his collar. He had lived in the neighborhood his entire life; and according to him, "It was the most boring place on Earth!"

James, on the other hand, had hair the color of fire with freckles to match. He kept his hair very short in a burr cut because he didn't like his hair. He was from the "country" and often went there to visit his grandparents. Sam had wondered what country he was from when they first met, but James just meant outside the city in one of the rural counties.

In the fall, the sequel to Sam's favorite movie series of all time — *Star Wars* — was playing at 2:00 PM at the Madison Theatre. Joey wanted to go with Sam to see it, but Sam begged his mother to let him go with his friends. She finally agreed.

On the following Saturday, the Fearless Five hurried down Pike Street to get to the theatre on time. They were eager to see *Empire Strikes Back* – again. The boys talked the entire way there about what they remembered from the movie, and they also talked their entire trip home about many of the exciting scenes in the movie that they had forgotten. This second time seeing the movie had met their expectation, and they were already anticipating a third sequel.

After the movie, the boys decided to shoot some hoops on the rooftop. They were still feeling pumped over the movie when somebody brought up the idea of having another campout on the roof. Alex was a bit squeamish about bats after his first nighttime encounter with them on the roof. "There's no way I'm going to the roof at night unless we find a way to keep the bats away," Alex exclaimed with a slightly higher tone. "And what about those bird thieves?"

As Alex rambled on, Dave suggested that a campfire might just be the trick to deal with the bats. "But how could we build a campfire on the roof?" he asked.

"We'll need a fireproof container and we'll need to keep it controlled," said Brian, being the cautious one.

"I know where we could get a big barrel," chimed in James.

"How do you suggest we get a big barrel up the stairs and out the window?" asked Sam in a disbelieving tone. "I don't think we can, but maybe we could use something not quite as big. What about a galvanized bucket or tub, if we can find one. One thing we must do is keep it small; otherwise, the neighbors will see the fire and call the police."

"Hey, I think we have one of those tubs!" said James. "My mom brought one back from Granny's to put flowers in. It's still in our shed. I'll bring it."

The boys planned the campout for a Friday night when Sam's mom and Joey were going to an open house at Joey's school. "We can plan it for 8:00-9:30. That way it will be dark and my mom won't be home till at least 10:00 PM." Sam told Dave. "If she sees a fire, she is going to freak out!"

And that's how the beginning of the end started.

* * * * *

Jenna overhead Sam and Dave talking about the campout one day as they were walking home from school. In typical Jenna fashion, she wanted to butt in when she heard some boys would be there.

"Maybe we could all have a party before you guys spend the night," Jenna said to Sam.

"I don't know. I need to ask the guys," was Sam's hesitant reply.

"It would be fun! I'll bring Holly and Jessica," Jenna replied trying to convince Sam about the party.

The next day Sam pulled Alex and Dave aside in gym class. He told them about the idea of having a boy-girl party with Jenna and her friends. They all agreed it could be fun and that it wouldn't interfere with their plans about the campout.

After Sam told Jenna the girls could come, she, Jessica, and Holly planned for the party almost as much as the boys. Of course, Jenna and Jessica were concerned about what to wear to a rooftop party with boys and how to fix their hair; but Holly was just along for the ride. The girls planned to pick up some chips and candy and to spend the night at Holly's following the party. They got it all arranged with their parents.

Sam had made Jenna swear to keep the party a secret from their mom. "It was just going to be a campout with the boys," he said. "You girls were the ones who turned it into a party!"

Jessica was in the same grade as Jenna, and they had been friends since Jenna moved to Covington. She had long auburn hair that she often wore with a headband, which pulled her hair back from her face. Except for the color of their eyes, Sam often thought she and Jenna looked a lot alike. They were typical girls who liked make-up and all the other frilly things girls like.

Holly was different. She was a year younger than Jenna, making her closer to Sam's age. She and Jenna had been in a couple of clubs together and had become friends. But they didn't hang out a lot like Jenna and Jessica did.

Holly had long blond hair and blue eyes. She generally wore her hair in a ponytail, and her glasses always seemed to be mid-way down her nose. She didn't wear pink bows, sequins, skirts, or dresses. Instead, she was usually dressed in jeans or shorts and a t-shirt. She was just different. Even her name was different!

On the day of the party, the Fearless Five carried the big galvanized tub up the stairs, through the window, and onto the roof. They positioned it between the shack and the outbuilding that jutted from the apartment in a way that prevented the neighbors from seeing it. Later that evening, they went to the roof about 7:00 PM. They brought food, music, and stuff for the fire. The girls came later and ended up being an awkward treat.

It was always a little windy on the roof, but that night it seemed even stronger. The boys decided to block the tub from the wind by putting some chairs around the bucket and draping a blanket over them.

When Dave started the fire, Jenna protested a bit about it; but Sam reassured her they knew what they were doing. Jenna kept nagging Sam about the fire, and he became angry. "Jenna, I'm not a kid and you are NOT my mother!" Sam retorted after Jenna asked about the fire for the third time.

"No, but I can certainly tell OUR mother!" Jenna huffed and then walked back to her friends. She seemed more interested in talking to Brian than worrying about the fire anyway.

After everyone arrived, they spread the drinks and snacks on a table and settled back in some chairs around the campfire to listen to the music. It was a nice autumn night so a fire was perfect — even if it was a small one. There were no other lights except the glow of the fire from the tub.

What would a campfire party be without a scary story? Alex thought. So, he began telling the girls that bats like to swoop down to pick up stuff from human hair. As he shared the story with elaborate detail, he demonstrated his point by pulling at the barrette in Jessica's hair. The girls' eyes got as big as the potato chips they were eating! Jessica shrieked and pulled away.

But Alex wasn't through. He went on to share the story about the thieves. But, of course, there were at least three or four of them; and they were big and gruff and they chased the boys on the roof. Then, he went over and stood by Jenna and put his arm around her shoulder. With a fearful tone in his voice, he said, "We don't know where they are or if they'll come back." Then he walked over and stood close to Holly. "We just always keep a close lookout for them," he said as he looked over Holly's shoulder. But Holly wasn't buying any of his tall tales! She just mumbled, "Whatever," and turned away from him.

Sam immediately liked Holly's reaction and her not-so-girly ways! She was wearing sneakers, a pair of jeans, a button-up hoodie, and t-shirt. Sam could see the picture of a bicycle peeking out from beneath her unbuttoned hoodie. It was then he remembered seeing her on the first day they moved into the neighborhood; she was the girl riding her bike that day.

"Holly, I like your t-shirt," said Sam trying to break the ice.

"Thanks, it's from one of the bike stores in Erlanger."

"I saw you riding your bike on my street the first day we moved in. Do you still ride it?" asked Sam.

"Yeah, I ride every chance I get."

"What kind of bike is it?"

"It's a Stingray; I like to freestyle.[19] Have you ever heard of that?" asked Holly.

"No, but it sounds totally cool! Where do you ride this freestyle?"

"Mostly, I just ride on the sidewalks or on the back streets."

"I'd like to watch you ride sometime," Sam said. "Maybe you could teach me to freestyle."

"Do you have a bike?" asked Holly. "We could ride together sometime."

But before Sam could answer, the guys called him back to their circle. They started teasing him about liking Holly.

Brian leaned over to James; and in a whisper loud enough for Sam to hear, he said with a teasing tone in his voice, "Sam wants to ride his bike with Holly." Then, James leaned over to Dave and whispered loudly into his ear in the same taunting way, "Sam wants to kiss Holly."

"Shut up, you freaks!" shouted Sam. He was so bummed about it that he walked over to the fire, shoving the chairs out of the way. He picked up some small pieces of wood and paper and aggressively threw them into the fire. Within seconds, the fire shot up over the top of the tub causing fire sparks and small, burning pieces of paper to shoot from the tub. The wind carried the sparks across the roof.

Before they knew it, the roof had caught fire in a couple of places. The girls started screaming and made a quick exit through the second-floor window. Since they already had permission to spend the night at Holly's, the girls went directly there. They promised each other never to say a word about being on the roof.

The boys kept trying to stomp out the flames, but they realized it was going to spread out of their control. Alex, Brian, and James yelled something at Sam and fled the roof too. Now alone, Sam and Dave didn't know what to do. When Sam remembered the birds, he quickly went over to release them. Bewildered, Sam and Dave realized the fire was out of their control, and they ran down the stairs and into the street for help.

Once on the streets, Dave and Sam heard sirens and knew help was already on its way. That's when the first police car pulled up. Their panic turned to both relief and anguish. Sam couldn't remember ever feeling quite like it. Panic, remorse, and fear welled up inside him. His stomach hurt all the way up his chest, past his throat, and into his ears!

Dave and Sam crossed the street and watched the fire trucks arrive. Within minutes, ladders and firefighters were everywhere. They watched tenants coming from the building as smoke continued to billow from the roof. Because the fire had not spread to the main building, it didn't take long for the firefighters to extinguish it.

"Thank goodness, it wasn't too bad," Sam said to Dave. This is a secret between friends. Right?"

"Friends forever," Dave said.

"Forever," Sam replied convincingly.

They decided it was best for Sam to spend the night at Dave's house but then play it cool for a while after that and not hang out. When they got to Dave's, Sam tried to call his mom to say he was fine and that he was spending the night with Dave, but there was no answer. *Maybe she's not home from the open house,* Sam thought. *Or, maybe she's out front with the neighbors. Either way, I need to go home.* He knew he had to return to his apartment to reassure his mother, or there would be even more grief of a different kind.

When he got back, he saw some of the tenants still huddled outside talking about that old man on the roof. They said that he must have started the fire and that the police were looking for him. Some other tenants claimed it was the hooligans, saying they had heard a commotion on the roof.

Sam felt the feelings of anguish returning to his chest. *What if they blame Jessie?* Sam thought. **His** guilt sickness lasted for days. Sam knew the fire could have been even worse, ending up hurting someone.

Sam's bird's-eye view of the rooftop was now just a painful reminder of very poor judgment. It was hard for Sam to look at the wet, gray glob of burnt wood, chairs, and wire cages. What didn't get burned got drenched. The birds were, of course, long gone. There was nothing left but remorse.

Sam couldn't take the guilt anymore. He was concerned that the police would find Jessie and arrest him for something he had not done. He had to tell his mom the truth about the fire — *Only me!* he thought to himself. *I can't take the chance that Dave will get in trouble. They might go harder on him since he is a foster kid.* He was firm that he wouldn't rat on Dave or the others. *After all, friends forever,* he thought. *I was the one who threw the wood and paper into the fire.*

One morning, about a week after the fire, Sam heard the fluttering at his window. It was B-52 and she had a note. It read, "Sam, courage lies within you. Jessie." After he read the note, he knew what he had to do. Sam knew his life as he knew it might be over, but he had to come clean! He couldn't let Jessie be blamed for something he had done.

Chapter 11: Facing the Music

Later that week, Sam walked bravely to his mom's bedroom and knocked on the door. As soon as he saw her face, he started to sob.

The week ahead was filled with meetings with officers at the police station, a court-appointed lawyer, and the pastor of Gram's church — at Gram's insistence. Sam got tired of telling his story, but he remained determined to keep his friends out of it. Finally, a hearing was scheduled in juvenile court.

Sam had never been to a courtroom. Now, he had to stand in one and, in front of strangers, give an account of what happened. The judge sat higher than others with what looked to be police officers guarding each side of the bench. There were two tables in front of the bench where Sam, his mom, and his court-appointed lawyer sat.

The judge called the case and asked Sam to come to the front of the bench. "Not too close," the policeman on the right said as Sam approached the judge.

There was a large circle of inlaid wood between the tables and the judge's bench — right in the center of the room. It had a big light that shone over it. The policeman pointed to the center of the circle and told Sam, "Stand there." It was all very official and structured. It didn't feel friendly at all. Sam noticed it was like standing in a spotlight and that he was center stage. He felt very small and insignificant.

His life flashed before his eyes. *It is over*, he thought as he stood dwarfed in front of the judge's bench.

The judge heard the scenario from Sam's lawyer, the police officer, the fire chief, and someone representing the building owner who chose not to appear in court. Then he asked Sam to tell his story. Sam's tears had all been spent by this point, and he told his story showing a degree of wisdom that even impressed the policeman on the right of the judge's bench. His mother was proud. He expressed his regret and added that he had learned a valuable lesson about building fires on tar roofs and acting impulsively in anger. He didn't name others who were at the party.

After his remarks, the judge went on and on about how Sam's actions had caused so much danger, disruption, and damage to property. By this time, Sam was sure that he would spend the rest of his life in prison—he just knew it. He thought the judge would never stop—solitary confinement came to Sam's mind. But then the judge finally concluded that it took a lot of courage for Sam to tell the truth. The judge looked at the police officer who had testified first. "Do you think this boy has learned his lesson?"

The officer replied, "Yes sir."

"Do you think he is a threat to the community in the future?"

The officer replied, "Judge, I think Samuel has deep regret for his actions, and he has told me he'd like to make up for it."

The weight of ten semi-trucks felt like it was being lifted from Sam's shoulders; he sighed with relief .... *Maybe at least solitary confinement is off the table,* Sam thought.

Next, the judge passed sentence, "Samuel, you are a lucky boy. The building owner is not pressing charges but instead asks that you learn a good lesson from this irresponsible behavior. You will be on probation for six weeks, and Officer Epstein will be your probation officer. You will complete 60 hours of community service — ten hours a week. You will assist in cleaning up the debris on the roof in addition to the community service. And you will report weekly to Officer Epstein to continue your lesson on the value of private property, fire safety, and many other things."

The judge then turned to Officer Epstein and said, "Officer, I want a full report of this young man's actions at the end of six weeks. If he acts up or violates any of these instructions in the meantime, you are to bring him back to this court immediately." Finally, the judge took a gavel and smacked it on his desk. A chill went up the back of Sam's neck and crawled across this head. Sam realized he had a close call with juvenile detention, and he was thankful for the judge's decision!

And that's how Sam spent the latter part of fall in 1982 — painting the park's swing sets, cleaning the park, and cleaning the fire trucks. Oh, and the firefighters' boots too! Then, there were the dinner dishes for life that were added to the sentence by Sam's mom.

Some days weren't too bad because Dave decided he should help. He knew that Sam had not ratted him out. "Friends forever," Dave told Sam on the first day he joined him on the sooty roof.

One day as Sam was on the roof cleaning up debris and soot, he found a clean feather lying near where the pigeon roost had been. He recognized it as a falcon feather because it looked just like the friendship feather Jessie had given him. He decided that an untarnished feather amidst the sooty mess was probably worthy of keeping so he stuck it in his back pocket.

Later that night, he took the feather from his pocket and ran his fingers across its soft edges. Finding it reminded Sam of Jessie's lecture on soul healing. *Is it a coincidence that I have found it, or is it a message about something more important?* Sam tried hard to remember what Jessie had said. *It was something about time for healing the hole in my heart and using my wisdom and courage to understand why my father is not here.*

He pulled a book on birds from his bookshelf. He had purchased it at the used book store on Scott Street when he was first fascinated with pigeons. As Sam was reading the book, he discovered that around the time he was born, the Peregrine Falcon was placed on the endangered species list, and several "hacking projects" were put in place to restore the species. As part of the hacking project, young hatchlings were nurtured until the time they could be released into the wild. These young falcons were released in urban areas, and Sam thought surely the feather he found must have been one from a falcon released in the Tri-State.[20]

After a few paragraphs, he read in print what Jessie had told him about falcons — they are natural predators and can fly at speeds of 200 miles per hour when attacking prey. The image of the falcon swooping down to attack the pigeon burned through his brain! Jessie's words about challenges followed the image, "Challenges will grab you by the throat and carry you off if you don't resolve them."

Sam stood at his window and tried to remember what Jessie had told him about finding his wisdom and courage to resolve his challenges. The window was cracked so he could hear crickets chirping off in the distance. A dog was barking on an adjacent street. He could hear traffic from I-75 as it hummed by. His eyes followed a firefly for what seemed like five minutes. He felt a sense of calm sweep over him, despite the last six weeks of embarrassment and hard work. *This is what Jessie meant about the healing sounds of Mother Earth. Stop thinking and just listen! Wisdom will come to you.* And it did— Sam knew that he had to have a conversation with his mother about his dad. *Someday,* Sam thought.

Officer Epstein spent more time than was required with Sam during those six weeks. He was young; and when Sam was finished with his probation duties, he would play basketball with Sam and his friends. As they continued to play, Sam got much better at shooting and handling the ball.

When Sam's probation period finally came to an end in December, Officer Epstein encouraged Sam to find a church basketball league he could play in through the rest of the basketball season. After talking to his grandmother, Sam found out that her church had a league. He asked Gram to help him meet the basketball coach, and she was thrilled to do it. Within a few days, Sam found himself on the basketball team and then started playing with them every Thursday night through March.

There were young men and older boys on the team so the younger team members didn't get to play that often in games. But, Sam stuck with it because it gave him a place to play. He enjoyed the practices. Before the season was over in March, he had sharpened his dribbling and his shooting. He could even make baskets from two-feet beyond the paint.

Chapter 12: Grit

Since his last birthday, Sam had grown two inches and put on some pounds. In August, as parents and kids usually do, Sam and his mom headed to shopping for school supplies. At the store, they were busy looking for pencils, protractors, calculators, composition books, and other items listed on the seventh-grade school supply list.

Sam heard a familiar voice, "Hi, Sam. Did you have a good summer?" Mr. Jones, the school's maintenance man, asked in a cordial greeting.

"Yeah," Sam said, still curious about the calculator he was buying.

But Sam's ears perked up when Mr. Jones said, "I heard we're looking for a few players for the basketball team this year. You should try out."

Sam's mom and Mr. Jones exchanged some small talk about extracurricular activities as Sam continued to explore the different types of calculators.

In the next aisle, they also saw Holly and her mom. The adults started comparing notes about needed supplies, and Sam and Holly had their own conversation.

"Man, it's good to see you! I heard you were doing community service after the fire. Is that all over? Are you excited about school starting, Sam?" Holly asked.

"Yeah, it's over and it wasn't too bad. I learned a good lesson about fire and tar roofs!"

"You can say that again," said Holly.

"I got to play a lot of basketball when I was doing the community service, and Mr. Jones was just telling me how they needed boys for the basketball team. I don't know if I'll try out or not for the school's team. I don't think I'm that good. It would be fun, though."

"You never know unless you try!" Holly said. She quickly added, "Hey, I wanted to ask you if you have a bike. On the night of the fire, you never got a chance to answer that."

"Yeah, I got one for Christmas a couple of years ago, but I think it needs some repairs. I'll have to get that done before I can ride it." They noticed their parents were getting ready to leave so they said their friendly good-byes and joined their parents.

Although Sam may have seemed uninterested in what Mr. Jones said in the store, he had heard every word. When he got home, he looked at himself in the mirror. *I am kind of tall — and quick on my feet,* he thought. Suddenly, Sam felt something he had never felt in mid-August — excitement about returning to school!

On a rainy day in September when Sam entered the schoolhouse door on his first day in seventh grade, he felt this year might be different. He would stay away from trouble. He would do his homework. And, he would try out for BASKETBALL!!!! But, as the day went on moving from class to class, his excitement fizzled out. All he had done during the day was write new assignments in his notebook. And the realities of school began to sink in.

Sam knew he had to keep up his grades to play basketball so he faithfully finished his homework each night. He worked on it as soon as he came home from school, and then he practiced basketball.

Sam's cousin Troy had told him once that dribbling with both hands was the key. And so, Sam decided to use the rooftop to practice. After Sam had cleaned it up from the fire, the owner of the building had fixed the roof and hung a better light. He even added a new basketball hoop and backboard. These improvements enabled Sam to practice into the night. Sam used it frequently to practice his shooting and dribbling to the basket.

As his basketball went through the new hoop for the first time, Sam was reminded of Jessie's dreamcatcher. The net looked a lot like the dreamcatcher's woven center, which was to catch the bad dreams and let the good dreams pass through. And Sam was dreaming of being a basketball star!

Sam talked Dave and Alex into trying out for the team with him. They were all a little concerned about one making it and not the other. Right up to tryouts, Sam didn't know for sure whether they were going to do it or not.

When tryouts came, Sam felt confident. As he entered the gymnasium carrying his book bag over one shoulder, he realized almost every boy in the class was there! That's when the doubting began. He wondered how many other boys were encouraged by Mr. Jones! The doubts about his ability continued as he took a seat like all the rest, avoiding the eyes of the other boys sitting on the bleachers.

The coach entered the room, blew a whistle, and yelled, "Listen up!" — and when Coach Cady yelled — you knew to listen! The rumble of clamoring voices ended abruptly — suddenly it got eerily quiet. Coach Cady had been coaching basketball at their school for at least 15 years and everyone knew him.

He started giving out instructions, "All you guys that are at least five foot and seven-inches tall go sit on the bleachers over there," pointing to the seats near the locker room doors. Sam wasn't quite five foot and seven inches, but close enough. He wasn't going to miss this opportunity. He hopped off his seat and followed the taller boys, and then he saw Dave and Alex among them. They huddled together throughout the rest of the tryout.

During that first week, the coach worked the boys hard to determine if he would have to recruit from the shorter boys who had left the gym. One of the first things he said to them when he entered the gym was, "Do you have the grit it takes to do the work?" In unison, every boy in the gym murmured, "yes;" and then over the next few weeks, they found out what grit meant.

There were six returning boys to the team from last year, meaning the coach needed a few new players. It didn't take long for the coach to sort those that he wanted; and Sam, Alex, and Dave were still on the roster!

Practice was hard — every day after school — sometimes till 5 o'clock. Some days there was extra work, too, like running laps or lifting weights. Afterwards, Sam had to walk the long route home, followed by eating supper, doing homework, and finally sleeping. Some days Sam wondered if it was worth it.

Then, one day the uniforms came — shiny red and white — just like that old hat hanging on the back of his bedroom door with the writing, "I'd rather be playing hooky." That day after class in the locker room before practice, Coach, as the boys called him, began throwing shirts to all the players. Sam's shirt had the number 24 on it; and he thought to himself, *Oh! This was worth it!* And so, day after day, Sam practiced and practiced for a chance to play in a game.

Right away, Coach Cady noticed Sam's ability to control the ball safely. He called him a "ball handler" and chose him to be one of the five starters — the point guard — not because he was a great shot, but because he could dribble to the right or left and out-maneuver most any guy on the team.

On the night of the first game, Sam started to enter the gymnasium door. He was so nervous that it's a wonder he even noticed it. Lying on a ledge near the door was a blue feather that immediately caught his eye. He quickly picked it up and stuffed it in the side pocket of his gym bag. He couldn't think about feathers now! He was too nervous. *Why does the first game have to be against St. Therese? — Those guys are giants!* he thought. *How will I ever get a ball around players that tall?*

In the locker room, Sam began to experience some anxiety with all the physical symptoms that go with it — his stomach ached and he felt dizzy and disoriented. He told the coach he was not feeling well; but the coach just explained that most players feel this way — like "knots in your stomach." Coach said it was adrenaline pumping, preparing Sam to do his best.

"It's your built-in mechanism for survival, Sam! Your mind is perceiving a challenge, and your body is reacting to it," Coach said. So, Sam just decided not to fight it! *Is this what Jessie meant when he was talking about facing challenges?*

Sam and the other five starters ran to the floor one at a time as their name was called. It was thrilling for Sam, Dave, and Alex to get to play in their first game in middle school. The bleachers were full, but there was no one there to watch Sam or Dave play. Alex's folks were sitting on the second row.

The buzzer sounded — the jump — the tip — and the game was off and running. It was a struggle for both sides to even make a basket. At half-time the score was tied at 17-17. In the locker room, Coach started breaking chalk on the blackboard. He told the team that the opponent would find the weakest link and run through it. He said, "Get out there and hustle — don't be afraid to sweat. And remember basketball is a team sport and that means we need all of you to play your best!"

With only seconds left in the game, St. Therese was ahead by one. While Sam was bringing the ball down the court, Coach gave the signal for him to call play #9. The purpose was to get the ball to Justin after a block was set by Alex to get him open—but Justin didn't get free enough to pass the ball to him—Sam had to improvise. He backed up a bit and waited to hear another call from the bench, but none came. Eighteen seconds remained in the game. Sam began to set up the play again as he came down the court, but at the last minute he got an idea— B-52 flies low and slow. He remembered how Alex could always find the open space, and he was in position.

Sam let the clock tick away until there were only ten seconds left in the game. He drove hard to the right, leaped in the air for a shot, but, instead, passed the ball back to Alex who was positioned perfectly with no one guarding him. Alex snatched the ball and just as quickly released it into a 15-foot perfect arch toward the basket. Although it took only seconds, it seemed like minutes! The players — both teams — held their breaths. Silence fell over the gym and then a loud uproar of clapping and cheering. He made it, and they won their first game!

Coming off the court and heading toward the locker room, the coach asked," Sam, what the heck was that?"

"It's called an assist, Coach," Sam said and smiled.

"I know that knuckle head!" the coach said as he tousled Sam's hair. At that moment while relishing in the glory of the win, Sam decided he liked school, and he especially liked belonging on the basketball team!

Sam was exhausted after the game so he went directly home and began to get ready for bed. For whatever reason, the notion of rules came to his mind. Following the hat incident, he was so mad about rules and boundaries for behavior. He had even watched Jessie live on the rooftop and thought about how FREE he was. But now, he could see that rules are important. *How else can we decide who wins and who loses? Yes, rules are important,* he thought, *but grit and Jessie's good common sense are important too.*

Sam noticed the feather on the side of his gym bag. He had more time to look at it now. This feather was different from others he had found. It was bright blue with a little turquoise. The unusual colors had attracted Sam to the feather and he had to pick it up. Even though Sam was tired and desperate to get some sleep, he took the time to put this beauty into his collection.

Sam had the time of his life winning and even losing games that year. He seemed to do a lot better in class and his friends thought he was COOL! For the first time, he felt like he was connected to something important at school. It also seemed to help with the bullying—or at least that's what he thought.

Sam wanted to tell Jessie about Coach, how he talked and listened to him. He wanted to tell Jessie everything—how the kids treated him now and, of course, about the St. Therese game. Sometimes, Sam would go to the roof, sit down on the lawn chair that lingered on the roof near his makeshift basketball hoop, and think about what Jessie would say.

Then came the big night of basketball honors. The school had a special program during a Friday-night basketball game where players' families were recognized. The family was awarded a t-shirt with their son's uniform number on it at half-time. Sam was a bit concerned, because his family had never seen him play. It wasn't that they weren't proud or interested, they just had too much on their plate already.

Sam beamed when he saw his mother, Gram, Jenna, Joey, and Troy stepping down from the bleachers when his jersey number was called. Gram held the t-shirt with the number 24 on it high in the air; other parents clapped and yelled Sam's name until his family got back to their seats. However, as most boys would, Sam wanted his dad there to see what he had accomplished. And Jessie was not there either, or so he thought. But Jessie was there, sitting unnoticed in the bleachers and smiling inside and out!

Things were different for Dave that night. Only one of his foster brothers came down when his number was called. To the surprise of Sam's family, Joey stood up too and followed Dave's foster brother down to the floor. That's when Jessie stood up too and followed Joey. He hadn't planned on it; but when he saw only the foster brother and Joey's unusual display of affection, he got up and joined them. Sam beamed from ear-to-ear to see Jessie and Joey supporting Dave. And, of course, all the team players yelled and whooped it up for Dave too. So that night, Dave's "family" was an African American, a Caucasian, and an Native American.

After the game, everyone on the team was giddy from the excitement of the game; and they decided to go to Alex's house. His parents had made an area in the basement for his dad to hang out with his friends, and they let Alex use it too sometimes. There was a TV and several couches and chairs.

There was also a small bar that was in one corner where Alex's dad kept some liquor. When Dave saw the liquor, he dared the guys to try some of it to celebrate. Dave tried it first, and as often happens, the other guys felt like they must meet the challenge. One by one they took their turns, all except Sam.

Dave, then, began pressuring Sam to try it as well. Sam didn't want to be the only chicken in the group so he tried it too. That started a night of "sampling" several different kinds of liquor from behind the bar. Since this was the first time many of them had drunk alcohol, they drank too much, and several ended up spending the night with Alex.

Sam ended up sleeping on the top bunk in Alex's room. Every time he raised his head off the pillow, the bed seemed to spin like one of the Star Wars spaceships! He was so sick to his stomach that he was afraid of puking, but he couldn't raise his head from the pillow to get to a bathroom. It was a miserable night.

The next morning Sam went home; but instead of going to his apartment, he went to the rooftop to avoid seeing his mother. He didn't expect that anyone would be there. He was wrong.

Sitting in a chair near where the shack used to be was Jessie. Having experienced a hangover himself on more than one occasion, Jessie immediately recognized Sam's problem.

"Hello, Sam. How are you feeling?" asked Jessie just to be irritating.

"To be honest, Jessie, I'm feeling pretty rough."

"Why?" questioned Jessie, knowing full well what the problem was.

Then Sam told him the story about sampling the alcohol and the miserable night he had on the spinning bed.

Jessie smiled inside because he was glad the night was miserable; and then he said, "Well, Sam, I need to tell you what the Shawnee elders used to tell our people. They believed an enemy (a serpent) would one day come to destroy us.

"When they saw the flag on the mast of the European ship in the harbor, they thought it looked like a snake's tongue — a serpent. And they thought surely the enemy had come. But later, when the elders tasted the sailor's rum, they declared, 'THIS is what will destroy our young men.'" [21]

And then Jessie confided in Sam about his own trouble with alcohol. "There was a time in my life when I started to drink alcohol to cope with my depression and loneliness. I made some friends at one of the local bars; and amidst the fun and laughter, one drink often led to six or seven. That's the trickster part of the serpent — you enjoy it. And I did, until one day I woke up on the stoop in front of my apartment instead of in it. It was a challenge to quit it. I felt like the falcon's claws were tight on my throat. I was no longer in control of my own mind and heart; the falcon had me and was carrying me off."

Sam was listening, but he was still distracted by what felt like the snake roaming around in his stomach. He managed to say, "What did you do?"

"I built the shack here and got the homing pigeons to remind me to use my navigation instruments — my wisdom and courage — wisely. A lot of things can interfere with the way our navigation instruments work; too much alcohol is one of them."

Jessie looked at Sam to see if he was listening and understanding, and he was — every word. Jessie concluded, "I guess 'the serpent' crosses all our paths at one time or another, and what we do with it is something every warrior must decide for himself. I hope when you face the serpent again that you will remember the spinning bed and the clutch of the falcon's claws!"

Sam just buried his head in his hands; the snake had begun to climb out of his stomach.

Chapter 13: Hello, is somebody there?

By the time Sam was in eighth grade, he had grown quite a bit. His mom trusted him to make good decisions, and she allowed him to navigate the neighborhood freely. He and Jenna had even taken over the after-school responsibility for Joey. He still hung out with the Fearless Five and there had been no more episodes with the serpent or its aftermath.

However, the unrest about his dad still lingered, and it became more apparent one day as he was passing an old building near his school. It had once been a brewery in the early 1900's; and according to Sam's mom, his grandfather had worked there for many years before it closed in 1966. There were stories about the strange things that went on at night in the old building on 12th Street. Sam had heard these stories from other boys in his school so he knew that the warehouse was a scary place that probably should be avoided. Some had even said it was the hooligan's hangout.

One afternoon, as Sam was walking home from school with Dave, he thought he saw B-52 enter a window on the north side of the old brewery facing Cincinnati. It was then he remembered that Jessie had told him he had created a roost for the pigeons in the warehouse. He hadn't seen B-52 since she carried Jessie's last note about courage after the fire; and he thought if it was B-52, Jessie might be there too.

Sam decided to check it out, but he wanted Dave to go with him. Sam had intended to give Dave a friendship feather like the one Jessie had given him ever since the family night basketball game last year. That was the night Dave only had his foster brother attend the game for him. Now seemed like a good time to do it.

Sam felt ashamed that he had always been so wrapped up in missing his own father that he hadn't even thought about how Dave must feel as a foster kid. He couldn't remember his real parents, and he didn't know if he had any real brothers and sisters. But, as Dave always said, he was grateful for his foster family.

Sam thought he'd make the friendship feather out of some of the feathers from his collection, but he needed some leather and beads. He asked his grandmother for some help. She asked the reason for these unusual things, and he told her what he was making and for whom. "That's nice, Sam. I think he will like it," Gram said with an approving smile.

After rummaging through some old things, she found a shirt with leather trim that she thought would work. She also found a couple of necklaces. When she handed them to Sam, she asked, "Will these work, Sam? I am just going to give them away."

"Those are perfect! Thank you!" Sam replied, and he decided to work on the friendship feather with his grandmother.

They tied two feathers together with the leather string. Next, they attached some of the beads from the necklaces. They chose just the right ones, and Gram was the one who did most of the attaching. When it was finished, they were both pleased with the outcome. Sam couldn't wait to give it to Dave.

When Sam saw Dave coming out of the school building the next day, he yelled, "Dave, wait up. I have something for you."

"What's up?" asked Dave.

"Oh, I have a couple of things I want to talk to you about."

"Okay," Dave replied, not knowing what to anticipate.

"Remember Jessie?"

"Of course! How could I forget Jessie?"

"When I first met him, he gave me a friendship feather. It meant a lot to me so I made one for you," Sam said as he handed the feather to Dave.

"That's totally cool. Did you steal those beads from one of Jenna's necklaces?"

"Close," Sam replied with a smile, not wanting to tell him where he got them.

"Well, I like it. Thanks," Dave said as he put the friendship feather in his sweatshirt's front pocket for safekeeping. "What's the other thing?"

Sam replied, "Well, Jessie told me one time he kept the birds in that old warehouse over on 12th Street during the winter, and I think I saw B-52 go in one of the broken windows. Do you think it might mean Jessie is there? I thought we could go check it out."

"I don't know, Sam. You know some people say that place is haunted, don't you?" Dave quizzed.

"I heard there was some deep stuff going on over there, but I haven't heard anything about it being haunted!"

"And, also, I heard it was the hooligan's hangout!" Dave quickly added.

Sam went on, "Well, that's just hearsay. I thought you liked the ghoul stuff, and I thought it might be cool to check it out for ourselves. And, who knows, we might find B-52 and Jessie?"

"I never considered you for liking paranormal stuff, but sure! Absolutely! When?" Dave responded excitedly.

"We could go over now," Sam said.

But Dave had a different idea. "Back up the train, Sab. You mean right now, in broad daylight. Someone might see us. That place is off limits. What's wrong with going over tonight about seven? It's dark by then. That's even better!" Dave said with a creepy laugh.

With a bit of hesitancy, Sam agreed; they knocked knuckles and then went their separate ways. Secretly, Sam thought he would have much preferred going during daylight hours.

"Meet you in front of the sign shop on Pike Street," Sam yelled back.

Sam hurried home where his mom was waiting for him with dinner on the table. Sam loved coming in the front door to yummy smells in the kitchen; and, tonight, it was beans and hot dogs over bread. Sam wanted to eat quickly, but his mom was all into "What was your day like" conversation so dinner took longer than expected. With a bit of guilt mounting in the back of his throat, Sam explained to his mom that he needed to go back to the gym for evening practice. "And I need to get my homework finished first," Sam said as he asked to be excused from the table.

His mom excused him from chores after dinner, making him feel even more guilty for lying. Sam raced through his homework, grabbed a jacket and flashlight, and fled out the door. "Mom, I'll be back by 8:15," he yelled. Little did his mom know that his "gym practice" was to find a bird.

Dave was there, as promised, in front of the sign shop on the corner – about three blocks from Sam's house. Fitting for the occasion, Dave was dressed in black from head to toe with a black hooded sweatshirt, black sweats, and even black shoes. "Sam, I need to tell you what I've heard about the warehouse. You need to decide if this is something you really want to do."

"How bad could it be?" scoffed Sam.

"I heard that when the brewery was operating there was an accident that caused a fire in one section of the warehouse. Three workers were trapped for three days because of some fallen debris. Even though the fire was not that extensive, their bodies were never found. Some say they still wander the warehouse looking for a way out."

"Seriously?! That's about as hokey as the circus' two headed calf! Let's go!" Sam replied as he headed toward the warehouse.

As they approached the abandoned warehouse, it looked even more eerie without the light of day or electric lights inside. Sam was relieved he had remembered a flashlight; Dave, on the other hand, had not. They made their way to the back of the building. Most windows were either badly cracked or broken out, making getting inside easier. What they had not anticipated was how high the windows were. But the boys, being boys, couldn't let this small challenge stop them. Dave decided to hoist Sam up far enough that he could reach the window frame. Once there, he removed some broken glass and reached inside to unlock the window latch. With hesitation, Sam slid inside, encountering a wall of spider webs as he moved forward.

"Where are you, Sab?" asked Dave from outside the window. "You have the flashlight, and it's dark out here."

I ought to leave you out there for not bringing a flashlight, Sam thought. Realizing he preferred Dave to be with him, he quickly stuck his head out the opening and whispered, "Why didn't you bring one, you blockhead?"

He braced his legs against the wall to give himself support. "Take my hand, Dave," he said quietly. With a slight tug, they both ended up standing on the 55 gallon barrels that were lined up against the inside wall below the window.

As they stood on the drums, they used the flashlight to scan the landscape before them. All they saw were lots of old wood, some equipment, and a lot of big open darkness.

"It feels like we're in the belly of a great big beast," Sam said to Dave.

"It is big," Dave said. "Come on, let's see what we can find."

Sam decided to spook Dave for not bringing a flashlight. After sliding down the barrels, Sam purposefully turned off the flashlight, dropped it, and asked Dave to help look for it. As Dave was crawling and patting around on the dirty floor, he started spouting frustrated comments about losing their only light. That's when Sam made his move. He picked up the flashlight and then quietly sneaked over near Dave. Just as he grabbed the back of Dave's shirt, he put the flashlight under his own chin and, with the ugliest face he could muster, flipped on the light but didn't say a word.

Dave turned around and jumped straight up, tripped back, and hit an empty drum so hard it sang out like an echo in a canyon. He let out a loud, "Darn it, Sam!"

By now, Sam was laughing hysterically, louder even than the echo of the drums.

After catching his breath, Dave turned around and said, "You scared the crap out of me, you jerk."

Sam couldn't stop laughing and fell back against the drum too. Dave reached out and grabbed the light and gave Sam a quick whack on the head with the butt of his palm. "Come on, Sam. This place gives me the creeps."

Sam looked over at Dave, smiled, and said, "Uh, duh. I thought you were into this deep stuff."

Dave was now in command of their only flashlight, and Sam watched it's beam as Dave made his way across the large warehouse floor. Quickly, Sam tried to catch up.

Then Sam heard sounds coming from deep in the darkness. "Dave," Sam said, "did you hear that?"

"What?" asked Dave.

"Up there! It sounds like something is moving. Turn the flashlight beam up there!"

"I'm not falling for another one of your tricks, Sam!"

"I'm not joshing! Listen."

When Dave heard it, the flashlight beam stopped moving, along with Dave. He was rethinking whether to go any further. But then Dave did as Sam directed and started scanning around the ceiling.

"It seems like something is breaking up the flashlight's beam. There! It did it again!" Sam said. "Did you see the shadow?"

Dave flashed the light all around them. Then he said, "I hear it! Look! There it is! There's the shadow! What is it?" He stopped dead in his tracks again. The flashlight beam went off.

"Turn on the light, Dave! Stop messing around!" Sam scolded Dave.

"I'm not. The battery has died, or worse!" yelled Dave. "I'm getting out of here!" and he started running back toward the window with only the light of the moon shining through it.

"Dave, wait, I'm sure it's nothing," he yelled; but still, he ran to catch up with Dave.

Before Sam could get halfway across the floor, he could hear Dave shouting, "Oh God, I won't look at dirty pictures; I'll take the blind man's garbage out from now on; I'll quit cussing." Then, all Sam heard was the sound of the drum as Dave leapt out the window.

Sam was now alone. It was pitch black. He called for Dave to "get back in here," but no response was heard.

Unsure of his footing yet too scared to go slow, Sam headed for the window. Over the sound of his feet hitting the concrete floor, Sam could hear what sounded like a squeaky door across the large room. He stopped, too afraid to move. It was eerily quiet. Suddenly, he could feel something or someone close beside him. He mustered the words, "Hello, is anyone there?" He said it again a bit louder, but no response came. As quietly as he could, Sam headed toward the window, now only visible by the moonlight.

He could feel the massive darkness behind him, ready to grab a leg or an arm. He turned to face it but saw nothing. He decided to back up toward the window. He quickly turned to scoot up the drums and climb out the window; and as he was hanging by his hands, he thought he heard a voice. He couldn't be sure if that's what he heard; but at any rate, he didn't care to hang there any longer and dropped to the ground.

With only the light of the few lamp posts along 12th Street, Sam rounded the corner toward Pike Street and ran right into Noah and his posse of hoodlums. "Oh, crap," Sam said out loud. Sam never said this word because his Gram once washed his mouth out with soap for using it. He was so surprised that it just slipped out.

"Well, well, well, who do we have here?" scoffed Noah.

Sam looked at Noah, but he was seeing a falcon. First the encounter with who knows what in the warehouse and now Noah—in real life, right in front of him. Trying hard to remember what Jessie told him about using his wits with bullies, Sam raised his hand for a quick wave and mumbled, "Hello."

"If it isn't Mr. Basketball!" chimed in Monty, one of Noah's friends as he walked over behind Sam.

Sam's heart started to beat faster, and his breath was shallow – high in his chest. He felt a little light-headed. He remembered Coach's words about the body's built-in mechanism for survival—flight or fight response. He couldn't decide which might be best.

"Hey, Sam," Noah said giving Sam a little push on his shoulder. "It's getting late, you know. Why are you over here by the warehouse? Are you still looking for birds? You know the warehouse is haunted, don't you?"

At that point, Sam got very anxious. He was now thinking karate. But, instead, he decided to just keep walking. "No, man, I don't have time for birds anymore, with basketball and all. But I must admit the warehouse looks a bit haunted." And he just kept walking.

They tried to have a little more fun with Sam about the haunted warehouse, but he just went with the "jokes on me" slant and kept walking.

"What's your hurry?"

"Dave and a couple of team members are waiting for me over there," he said as he pointed to the dim light on one of the benches in front of the sign shop. Now Sam did not want to run—that would look cowardly. But he did walk with haste. All the way to the bench, Sam listened for footsteps behind him. Had his plan worked? He was afraid to turn around to find out. He just kept walking. As he got closer to the bench, he saw an illuminated t-shirt with a skull and cross bones on it. "Rock n' Roll" was scrawled across the bottom in red print that looked like dripping blood.

 The freaky skull-like face was glowing and shaking. Then, Sam heard Dave shout, "Look out!" The shirt jumped up and started to move toward Sam.

Sam was confused. Having just come from his close encounter with Noah and gang, Sam started running toward the bench where the t-shirt was, "Are they after me?"

Dave expected him to be running in the opposite direction away from the shirt. Baffled by Sam's question, Dave peeked out from behind the shirt and asked, "Who?"

"You, crazy nitwit! Noah and his friends are over there!"

Now Dave was confused! "Where?"

"By the hardware shop. They stopped me by the corner! Let's get out of here!" His heart was pounding harder, and he did not understand what Dave was trying to pull with his t-shirt. "What are you doing without your shirt on, anyway?" Sam asked in an unbelieving tone.

"I was trying to scare you," said Dave.

"I think we've had enough scare tonight, Dave. Let's go home," said Sam.

"Fine with me! What do you think that was in the warehouse?" asked Dave as they walked toward Lee Street.

"It was scary, whatever it was! I think we need to keep this adventure to ourselves. Promise, Dave?" asked Sam.

Dave replied, "I swear on my mother's grave I'll never go back to that place, and I won't tell a soul we were there!" When they got to Lee Street, they parted ways to go to their separate homes, each hurrying to get out of the darkness.

Chapter 14: Defining Moments in Time

Sam and Dave didn't think about what they had seen and heard in the warehouse for quite some time. They were busy with eighth grade graduation and transitioning to high school. Sam also worked sometimes as a caddy at a local golf club, which kept him busy, especially with his basketball schedule. Dave also worked from time to time helping his foster dad in his hardware store.

Soon after school began for their ninth-grade year, they learned they had made the junior varsity basketball team. It was only the two of them and a guy named Marty as the three new players.

It was a sad time for Sam and Dave in one way. For the first time since Sam, Dave, and Alex had become friends in fifth grade, the three musketeers were split up! The coach had chosen Marty over Alex because he was taller, leaner, and faster. He could dribble in and out and around most players, something that Alex had not mastered.

Marty's family was from the south, and he still had a bit of a southern drawl. Despite the age difference, he seemed to fit in well with the older members of the team.

Occasionally, the varsity players would assist the coach during junior varsity practice; and it was during one of those practices that John, the captain of the varsity team, decided it was time to initiate the three new players: Sam, Marty, and Dave. One day following practice, John pulled them aside. He told them their initiation was scheduled for the following Friday night. They were to meet him and some of the rest of the guys on the varsity team at the old warehouse on 12th Street. And then he added, "You know that place is haunted, don't you?"

Dave and Sam's ears perked up when he mentioned haunted warehouse, knowing what they had experienced last spring. They also wondered just what "initiation" would mean, but they just replied in unison to John, "We've heard."

The following Friday after sixth period Geometry class, John pulled Dave aside. "It's all set up. The other starters and I are meeting tonight at 9:00 PM by the hardware store. Make sure you tell Sam and Marty; don't be late!"

When Dave told Sam, the first thing out of his mouth was, "I thought you swore on your mother's grave never to go back there!"

"My mother's not even dead—or that I've heard anyway!" Dave huffed. "We have to go; that's all there is to it!"

They left it at that and went their separate ways, but Sam was grumbling as he went, "I'll be there."

Later that evening as Sam walked toward the rendezvous point, he had a sinking feeling in the pit of his stomach about things going badly. He was thinking about the voice he heard the last time he was there. Was it Jessie or someone else? And exactly what kind of initiation would it be?

He arrived for the rendezvous promptly at 9:00 PM, as planned. Standing in front of the hardware store were the starters on the varsity team, John, Rob, Larry, Mike, and Randy. Dave and Marty were also there. John and Rob were the only seniors on the team's starting five. The juniors were Larry, Mike, and Randy. Even though there were other players on the varsity team, it was the starting five that planned to carry out the initiation.

As they neared the warehouse, John yelled, "This is it guys! Are you ready for some fun? We need to move quietly from here and go around to the back of the warehouse. Who has the flashlights?"

Three guys flipped on lights.

"Turn those off, you pea brains," said Mike. "Someone will see them."

They moved closer to the back window with the stealth of a cat burglar. At the window, John paused to tell them, "Now, there was one guy that didn't make it through the initiation, but he was just a chicken. I'm sure you guys will be just fine." Sam, Marty, and Dave looked at each other with no expression on their face. They were afraid to show any expression for fear their mounting trepidation would shine through, and they would look cowardly.

John hoisted Rob up first; and then one-by-one they climbed in. Once inside, John told the guys to flip on their lights. Mike came prepared. He pulled out his big 15-volt camper flashlight that gave quite a bit of light and pointed it all around the ceiling. He was especially looking for creepy, flying things.

Seeing none, John and Mike began to lead the teammates back through the maze of heavy equipment, empty crates, and loading skids. Sam could hear Marty asking John questions about the building: What was it used for? What is it used for now? Is it empty? Are there any rats? Finally, John said, "Marty, shut up."

The boys got to a part of the warehouse where Dave and Sam had never been. They were walking shoulder to shoulder, and their eyes followed the flashlight beam as Mike moved it back and forth around the landscape. They were anticipating the appearance of the menacing shadow that they had seen last spring. But all they saw in the light beam was a wooden stairway that jutted off to one side. Mike let the light wander up the stairs until it stopped at a loft at the very top of the warehouse.

Hanging out from the loft floor was a three-sided cage held by pulleys with ropes that reached to the warehouse floor—a dumbwaiter—probably used to move heavy objects from floor to floor.

"Hold that light there, Mike. Everyone, wait up!" said John as he motioned to several of the boys to gather near the staircase. And then pointing to Marty, Dave, and Sam, he added, "This is your initiation. You guys have to ride in that cage from the floor to the ceiling. It's what all new members on the team have to do!"

"That's about 30 feet," Marty said with hesitation in his voice.

"We've all done it! It's safe," scoffed Larry.

Then Dave decided to play the "big guy." He quickly responded, "What this calls for is trust in your teammates to hold you up by the ropes. I trust you guys, and I'll prove it. I'll go first, but I want Mike and Larry to handle the ropes.

Everyone except Mike and Larry began climbing the staircase. The two boys stayed on the floor inspecting the ropes and getting ready to maneuver the lines.

As Dave looked down over the warehouse from the 30-foot perspective, however, he said, "Wouldn't it be wise for us to test this thing out first before anyone gets in?" He had begun to wonder just what the initiation was.

Sam and Marty agreed, but the older guys yelled out, "Chickens! It will work just fine! We've done it before."

Still, Dave insisted. Everyone looked around to find something with some weight that they could use to test the pulley; and, eventually, one of the guys yelled out that he had found a crate with some old magazines in it. Dave tossed it in the metal cage and yelled down to hike it up and then lower it down. When it reached the bottom safely, John said, "What did we tell you? It works just fine. It always has."

Satisfied with the test run, Dave hopped into the crate. With one big push off, he went flying into the open space, whooping and hollering all the time. After Dave's turn, he looked at Sam and said, "You're next, buddy."

Sam called for Rob and Randy to handle the ropes for him. When they were in position, he reached out over the loft and grabbed the cage. He climbed aboard and with the help of John, he swung the cage off the loft. Rob and Randy began working the ropes which lifted and lowered the cage. "Woohoo!" yelled Sam and the boys cheered.

Marty took his turn too. Like the other boys, he jumped from the loft onto the cage's floor. When his feet landed in the cage, it swung high into the open space. He could tell the boys on the floor were raising him higher; but he wasn't too bothered by the height of the cage as it climbed toward the ceiling. Even though he didn't mind the ride, he was not that eager to repeat the experience so he let all the other guys get in line in front of him. He only rode in the cage once.

The pulley creaked and moaned as the dumbwaiter moved back and forth in the darkness. In time, each member, new and old, took a turn. With each run, they became more confident throwing the cage out from the loft. Some took more than one turn. The boys tending the rope pulled so hard that their feet left the floor from the pure weight of the cage as it swung back and forth. The fun part was trying to lift the cage to the ceiling as quickly as they could once it was launched. Each launch was wilder than the one before.

John noticed Marty standing in the loft, but hesitant to ride again. He decided it was time to get on with his prank. John hollered out, "Marty, take one final ride! We need to get out of here."

Marty followed the command to catch the last ride and jumped in the cage. He was ready for this night to be over. Once the cage was released from the loft, John motioned to the guys on the rope to lift the floating cage high in the air near the ceiling and tie it off. John called out from the floor, "Hey Marty, we're going to tie these ropes off down here now. There's not too much to be afraid of. I'm sure the haunted warehouse is just a made-up story, but I hope you're not afraid of bats."

Marty laughed at what he thought was a joke; but when the boys began leaving the room, he yelled, "WAIT!" What are you doing? You can't leave me up here in this cage. How will I get down?"

"We'll be back in the morning to get you. It's just a rite of passage for the youngest player on the team — to spend the night in the warehouse on 12th Street, alone, in the dark, with the bats, and suspended high into the air. We know you can do it, buddy," reassured Rob.

At this point, Dave and Sam were in a dilemma. Do they go with the older boys or stay and help Marty get down? Dave made his decision quickly and whispered to Sam, "I'm getting out of here. I don't want to end up in there!"

And with that, Marty, suspended high above the warehouse floor, watched the beams of the flashlights head toward the front of the warehouse. That is, all except one. Sam was still in the loft and now had a pretty good idea of what the night would bring for Marty — and it wasn't very good.

In a moment that seemed like forever, Sam was torn about what to do — leave, lower the ropes (which Sam would have to do by himself), or stay with Marty. A flash of the torment Sam had felt with Noah crept over him. But the pressure of being accepted as a team member was too overwhelming. He decided to just take the middle ground, toss his flashlight to Marty, and reassure him that they would be back early in the morning.

As Sam hurried to catch up with the team, he could hear Marty crying out for them to return. But despite the guilt, fear, and even sympathy he felt, he left anyway.

As Sam dropped from the window frame at the back of the warehouse, all the guys were laughing and discussing whether they should sneak back in and give Marty a fright. They decided it would be better to just leave him alone — in the dark. Finally, John said, "Just meet us back here in the morning at 8:00 a.m. to get him down."

"Okay," they all mumbled and went their ways.

After the team left Marty, they split up and went their separate ways. Sam went home too; but his unrest persisted — he couldn't get the sight of Marty suspended in the cage or the sound of his plea out of his head. Neither could he forget about the shadow and voice he heard the first time he and Dave were there. *What if something or someone REALLY did hurt Marty?* Sam thought.

Sam hoped sleep would help him forget about what he had done. But two hours later, he was still not asleep. He looked at the clock. It was 12:05 AM.

Sam tossed and turned, getting up to go to the kitchen for a glass of milk, fiddling with his feather collection — nothing helped. He looked out his window onto the roof below. The light was casting a shadow across the new shiny backboard that had been installed to replace the one that had burnt. Even though Jessie never owned up to installing it, Sam knew he was the one because whoever did it kept the "Friends Forever" sign beneath it. That seemed to be like Jessie.

Sam finally went back to bed. As he lay there, his restlessness persisted. In what seemed to be somewhere between sleep and awake, Sam dreamed he was in a building that was on fire. A firefighter was carrying him down a flight of stairs. The smoke was heavy, and Sam was almost unconscious. He could tell he was at the point of death. To save him, the firefighter took off his mask to share his oxygen with him. When he did, Sam could see his crystal blue eyes. They looked just like his dad's eyes. The dream was so vivid that Sam leapt from the bed, still asleep. When he hit his head on the wall, he awoke.

He was sweating and his heart was pounding. He looked around him. His room's familiar surroundings snapped him back to reality. He realized he had awakened from another bad dream. Sam shivered as he remembered the crystal blue eyes of the firefighter — his dad's eyes — and how they had startled him so.

Then the image of Marty in the cage came bursting into his head. *What happened tonight was not fun!* Sam thought. *It was wrong! And I participated! I could have saved Marty.* At that point, Sam was completely awake. "It's not too late!" he said out loud. Joey stirred in his bed but didn't wake up.

Sam got up immediately to dress so he could head back to the warehouse. He finally found the clothes he was wearing earlier. He picked up his shoes from near the bed. As he lifted the first shoe toward his foot, a feather fell from it and drifted toward the floor.

Sam closed his eyes hoping he didn't see it, but no such luck. It was still there. *It doesn't look like one from my collection. Where did it come from? Is the feather a message? Is Marty hurt?* Sam thought. In his mind, Sam envisioned finding only a bloody mess in the dumbwaiter, for surely the menacing shadow must have already done something unimaginable to Marty.

He shook his head, put on the other shoe, and placed the feather on his dresser. *I can't think about that now*, he thought. He closed the door to his bedroom quietly. After picking up another flashlight from the kitchen, he made it out the apartment's front door without waking anyone.

When Sam arrived at the warehouse, he realized that he had not planned very well for getting back in. With a few running leaps, he managed to drag himself up to the window ledge. While climbing through it, the flashlight dropped to the ground — outside the warehouse — and he fell onto the barrels resting just inside. "Crap," he said out loud, unabashedly.

Without any light, it was hard for Sam to navigate through the maze of the warehouse. He no longer heard any noise out of Marty.   He was feeling his way along the old crates and machinery, hoping to get a glimpse of Marty's flashlight beam and hoping not to run into the thing that he had encountered last spring. The spaciousness of the dark warehouse was crushing. The dust that had been stirred up earlier was getting stuck in his throat. Now that he was alone he could hear only the sounds that the old steel and wood structure made as if breathing in the expansive darkness.

He yelled out to Marty but there was no answer. *Oh my God, he is dead!* Sam thought. At that very moment, something or someone grabbed both his arms and pulled him toward a shadowy corner.

Sam struggled with his captor and managed to say, "Who are you and what do you want?" There was no answer. Sam yelped as his captor yanked on his arm. It was one of those times when one realizes that life as you know it may be over. Sam tried to adjust his eyes to see what fierce creature or deranged lunatic had captured him. The clutch on his arm tightened as it pulled him into a darker enclosed space. Sam could feel its walls around him. *Surely,* Sam thought, *I'll be the next missing kid from the neighborhood – the next face on the milk carton! My lifeless body will land in some cold, dark hole next to Marty's.*

Then Sam heard Noah's voice, "You stupid jerk!"

Sam was somewhat relieved it was Noah and not an escaped convict. He managed to say, "I know, but I'm back. I need to get Marty down, NOW!"

But instead of saying anything about Marty, Noah and another bully just pushed Sam into an even darker room and locked the door when they left. The room was pitch black, and Sam was left alone for at least 10 minutes. To Sam, it felt more like 60 — long enough for his mind to conjure up all sorts of concern about what was going to happen to him when they returned. *Was it Noah's gang I heard last spring when I was here? Is this their hangout? What are they going to do to me? What are they doing now? Why didn't Marty answer me? What am I going to do if they DON'T return? Is this place haunted?*

Finally, Sam heard someone coming. His body flinched in anticipation of bodily harm. He felt around the room looking for something he could use to protect himself. He heard the door unlock, and then a light went on.

Noah, Monty, and another friend Sam didn't know were standing in the doorway. *Oh boy, this isn't going to be good*, Sam thought.

With the light on, though, Sam could see his surroundings. He saw things Jessie used to have in the shack on the rooftop. There were some photos, a cot, a new dreamcatcher, and the Purple Heart Medal. The first thing out of his mouth was, "How did you get these things? Is Jessie here?" But before Noah could speak, Sam demanded, "Where's Marty? Is he still in the dumbwaiter?"

"He's long gone. We got him down over an hour ago," said Noah. "He was scared to death. What you guys did to him was very wrong! You need to make it up to him."

"I will," replied Sam shamefully.

That's when Jessie came into the room.

"Oh, my gosh, Jessie, you are here!" Sam said with a sigh of relief.

"Sam, I'm sure you can't be proud of yourself or your friends after what you guys did to Marty. But, I am proud of you for coming back. I would expect nothing less from one of my warriors."

"I am so ashamed of it, Jessie," replied Sam as he dropped his head. Then he asked Jessie, "Did you help get Marty down?"

"No, you can thank Noah and the gang for undoing what you and your friends did. I was busy with the bird thieves a couple of blocks from here. I had no idea Marty had been left in the warehouse."

"What? Where are the thieves? Did they get B-52? Are they squab farmers? Are they gone?" asked Sam.

"Yes, they are gone. And no, they didn't get B-52; and no, they were not squab farmers. They wanted to steal B-52 for racing," said Jessie. "I had to convince them that they were not going to be taking her back to Texas. Remember what I told you about outwitting people who aim to hurt you? I realized that I would have to outwit them."

"How did you do that?" asked Sam.

"That's not important now. It's late and you boys need to be getting home," replied Jessie. "But before you go, what can we all do to teach the boys on the varsity team a good lesson about pranks?"

The boys started plotting and they did, indeed, arrive at a plan to teach the varsity team members a lesson about hazing.

Chapter 15: The Lesson

After the boys had arrived at a plan to teach the varsity players a lesson and before Noah left the warehouse, Sam stopped him to say, "Noah, thanks for getting Marty down. I need to tell you, though, I was a little afraid that I was going to end up in something worse than the dumbwaiter!"

"If it was up to me," said Noah, "you would have."

Sam gulped and Jessie chimed in, "Noah, his friends, and I became friends after his last encounter with you in the park, Sam. He was working with me tonight to outwit the bird thieves. That's when they found Marty."

Noah looked at Sam and grinned proudly as if saying, "I'm his favorite warrior now!"

Sam twisted his mouth in a grimace. And, most satisfied with himself, Noah and his friends left.

Then Jessie turned to Sam to say in a stern, fatherly voice, "Sam, this time no one got hurt because you just went along with the crowd. You let the pressure of your peers interfere with your navigation instruments. Next time you might not be so lucky. A man knows what is right and what is wrong in his heart and is not persuaded by others to abandon it. Remember what I told you about your internal compass — the wisdom and courage the Creator has given you? Next time you get in a situation where your friends are pressuring you to do something that you know is wrong, use your instruments wisely!" Sam hung his head in embarrassment, and then left to get a few hours of sleep.

He got up extra early for a Saturday morning and went straight to Marty's house as planned. Marty was not very happy to see him! "Man, I am so sorry! I didn't know they were going to do that, and I did go back for you!"

Marty looked at Sam with an "I could kill you" look. Then, in one quick move, he whacked Sam on the back side with his foot — not easy, but hard, really, really hard! Then, pointing a finger almost up Sam's nose, he said, "Don't you *ever* do something like that again to me or anybody! It was mean, and I did not deserve it."

"I know," Sam said. "You can't believe how sorry I am, Marty! Trust me, I learned my lesson! And we want to teach the varsity team players a lesson too about hazing. Do you want to help?"

"What are you going to do?" quizzed Marty.

"We were supposed to go back to the warehouse to get you down at 8:00 am, but you're not going to be there — obviously! Instead we want them to find an empty cage, and wonder where you are. They may call here. Just don't answer the phone. We want them to think something bad happened to you. We want them to worry. I'll try to keep them looking and wondering till noon."

"I'm in!" said Marty, "as long as I don't have to go back to the warehouse! Someday, I'll tell you what I saw there."

"Seriously? I want to hear that!" replied Sam as he left to return to the warehouse.

At 8:00 a.m., when Sam got to the warehouse, the varsity team players and Dave were already there. Noah, his friends, and Jessie were in Jessie's room hiding. The boys entered as they had done before.

"Oh, Marty. It's time to wake up," John yelled out almost in song.

There was no answer. He yelled again. No answer. When they got to the steps to the loft, they saw the dumbwaiter suspended high above the floor — just as they had left it. John and a couple of other guys yelled again. No answer. Dave looked at Sam, but Sam was not letting on that he knew Marty wasn't there.

John and Mike ran to the top of the stairs to try to see in the suspended dumbwaiter but they couldn't see anything. They yelled again, and again. No response.

They returned to the floor with an ashen expression. "He's not answering," said Mike.

"Oh, he's just playing with us," said Larry. Let's just get the dumbwaiter down. You'll see."

Rob and Larry started to work the ropes to lower the cage. As it crept toward the floor, John yelled out again. No answer. Finally, the empty cage landed on the floor.

Rob looked at Larry. Larry looked at John. Dave looked at Sam. No one had anything to say.

"He figured out how to get down," Larry said.

"He couldn't have. There is no way!" scoffed John

"Then what happened to him?" questioned Dave with a forlorn look on his face.

"Someone had to help him," said Larry. "Sam, you were the last one here. Did you help him?"

"I couldn't have worked the ropes alone! He was in the cage when I left," retorted Sam.

"John, we need to call his house and ask to talk to him," said Rob.

"That's a good idea. Where can we find the closest phone?" asked John.

"There's one on the corner of Pike and Lee Streets. You can go there. We'll wait here," directed Mike.

John quickly ran to the phone booth and called Marty's house. His mom answered but said Marty was not home.

"Do you know where he is?" asked John.

"He was supposed to spend the night with Sam," said Marty's mom.

John got a sinking feeling in his stomach as he thanked her and said goodbye. Then, he returned to the warehouse. Once inside, he said to the guys, "He's not there."

They all looked at each other with disbelieving eyes. They didn't know what to do or where to turn. That's when they heard the door of Jessie's room — the squeaky, creepy door — open, ever so slowly.

"What's that?" said Rob.

"I don't know," said Dave. "But once when Sam and I were here, we saw some mighty freaky things."

They waited for more noise. That's when Noah released the birds from their roost in the top of the warehouse and they swooshed by all the boys as if in some planned attack as they made their way out the open window.

The boys ducked, and wailed their arms above their heads. Some boys even let out an "EEK" as they swatted at the birds.

Once the birds had passed them, they saw a large shadowy figure approaching them. It seemed like Dave shrunk three inches as they all backed up. From the shadows, they heard a strange horn blow. Then a voice started chanting something they couldn't understand. It was a creepy chant and other figures joined him in the shadows. No one could tell if they were of this world or not.

The boys had backed up trying to get closer to their exit. When they got close enough, Dave turned to run away. That's when Jessie stepped into the beam of light that was filtering through a window high in the ceiling. He was wearing a long dark cloak-like thing with feathers and beads. He blew the fox horn[22] again. Noah and gang stayed in the shadows. Sam thought to himself that it actually looked like some kind of supernatural entourage. He smiled quietly on the inside as he watched Jessie's performance, and the boys reactions. Even Dave didn't recognize him at first.

John was mumbling curse words under his breath and Larry had positioned himself behind Dave.

Then Jessie spoke, "Marty is safe. There's no need to look for him anymore here. Go home and don't come back here, or you might end up in the dumbwaiter. You know tricks like the one you pulled on Marty are wrong," Jessie said with an authoritative tone. That was enough for all of them. They turned and bolted from the window.

Once safely outside, they began the chatter about who the big man was — or if he was even real. Both Dave and Sam kept quiet about Jessie. They wanted the others to be impressed by his commanding presence.

It was getting close to noon, so Sam suggested they go by Marty's to see if he was home. And, that's where they found him — watching Saturday morning TV and eating Sugar Pops. And, despite many pleas to find out how he got down, he, nor Sam, never told.

Chapter 16: The Feather of the Red-Tailed Hawk

In the spring of Sam's ninth grade year, he noticed Holly was still riding her Schwinn Stingray to school. He decided to ask her if he could walk home with her one day after school. She agreed so the very next day, Sam was waiting for her by the bicycle rack. He found, though, that it was hard to keep up with her because she kept jumping off curbs and over puddles in the sidewalk.

"Slow down, Holly, I can't keep up with you," Sam teased.

"Then ride your own bike to school and maybe you'll be able to!"

"I might just do that!"

After Sam left Holly, he went straight to Gram's garage to get his bike. It was a 20" so he thought he could still "fit." Because it had been sitting for a while, he had to roll it to the gas station to get the tubes fixed. He decided to wash it while he was there. The next day he rode his bike to school; and many days after that, he and Holly rode many places together.

Sam's mom questioned his new interest in his bike; but he explained, "It's just easier to ride to school than to walk." Of course, Jenna blabbed about Holly one night when Gram and his mother were both at the table. Sam's face turned ten shades of red!

Since Sam saw Holly almost every day, they became very good friends. She even walked to the theatre on Madison Street to see the movie Ghostbusters with Sam, Dave, and Alex.

On one of those rare afternoons when Sam had nothing to do, he noticed there was activity on the roof again. He saw Jessie and decided to join him. As he got to the second-floor window, he couldn't help but remember the night of the fire and his quick exit from that very window. He just shook his head a bit in disgust, regret, and disbelief that he could have been so stupid.

On the roof, Sam found Jessie sitting in a newer lawn chair. It looked odd to see the roof with the old tattered chairs, the lopsided shack, the clothesline, and the bird cages gone. When Jessie saw Sam, he raised his hands toward the sky. Sam didn't know quite what to think of that gesture, but he approached Jessie's chair despite his uncertainty about his reception.

"Bezon,[23] my boy! That means 'Good morning' in Shawnee, Sam," Jessie explained.

"Chief!" responded Sam in a familiar, yet kidding way.

"What have you been up to, Sam? Anymore close encounters with ghostly creatures?"

"No sir, not since the last one; but since you brought it up, I'd like some answers from you about that night."

"What would you like to know?" asked Jessie.

"How did you use Noah and his friends to outwit the thieves?"

Then Jessie told Sam about a very complicated scheme to keep B-52 safe and away from thieves and to get the gang members to do something positive for a change. "Sam, Officer Epstein and I are very good friends. He's helped me keep in touch with you over these last few months. That day, he told me he had heard thieves were in the neighborhood to find and steal B-52. He also said they were going to sneak in the warehouse to get her when I was not there.

"The very night you guys went to the warehouse for your initiation, I got a call to sit down with one of the thieves to discuss a deal. I figured it was a meeting to lure me away from the warehouse so the other thief could sneak in to get B-52. I knew I was going to have to outwit them. They were not going to leave us alone."

Jessie continued, "For quite some time, I had been talking with Noah about changing his ways and trying to get him and his friends into some positive things. This gave me an opportunity to help him along with that.

"After getting the call from the thief, I told Noah and his friends about the thieves' plan to steal the bird. Then, I asked him to help me keep the thieves from stealing them. I told him I'd give them some burgers and shakes and $20 to split if they'd guard the warehouse until 11:00 PM.

"Noah agreed and his gang sat just outside the front of the warehouse to watch for the thief. They heard a commotion and saw your teammates sneaking to the back of the warehouse. When they got around back, they watched you guys enter in the back window. Knowing they couldn't leave their post, they returned to the front and stayed there until the thief showed up. They ran him off with the help of Officer Epstein who was parked in his cruiser nearby, at my request.

"After the thief was gone, they heard you guys leaving and then they heard Marty yelling. That's when they went into the warehouse. And you know the rest of the story."

"I'm glad it worked out that way. I wanted to get Marty down, but I'm not quite sure how I could have managed that by myself. Aren't you afraid the thieves will come back," asked Sam.

"I told the thief I was meeting that B-52 was old and wasn't that fast anymore. I convinced him that she wasn't worth the trouble. I also promised to give him a couple of hatchlings when I see a good one," replied Jessie.

"So, everything turned out okay that night, I guess," concluded Sam.

"You know that night, with just a little planning, ended up with a lot of wins. Noah and gang did something positive; you learned a valuable lesson; and, the thieves did not get B-52. That's a jackpot, I'd say!"

"Yeah, everyone won except for poor Marty."

"He survived," said Jessie.

Then Sam decided to change the subject. "Did you come to the roof to see if I had ruined the roof again?"

"No, just testing these old legs to see if I can still make it up here. It is difficult for me to get through the window now. I've been using the warehouse sometimes to take care of the pigeons. Of course, it's a good thing I moved the pigeons' loft," he reminded Sam with a glance in his direction.

"Even though I wasn't seeing you every day, I did keep an eye on you, especially after you damaged the roof of my building."

Sam's eyes opened wide. He did not know it was Jessie's building.

"Yeah, Sam, I own this building you almost burned down! Why do you think the owner didn't show up in court to press charges?"

"I did wonder about that. Did you install the new basketball hoop, too?" asked Sam.

"Yes, I knew you were playing ball and needed a better place to practice. The new flooring and the basketball backboard with hoop and net were chosen to give you that place."

"Well, thank you. It has been great!" Then, out of the blue, Sam said, "I met a girl."

Jessie didn't expect to hear that from Sam, and his ears perked up. He smiled and responded, "Well, who is she? What's she like?"

"Her name is Holly and she's not your typical girl. She rides BMX bikes, and she's as good at it as most of the boys!"

"Is she pretty?"

"Oh, Jessie! I guess so," Sam replied a bit embarrassed; and changing the subject said, "I like the new floor on the roof—more fireproof!" he said with a laugh.

"Yeah, after the fire we had to repair the roof and fix some broken windows."

"It took me days and a lot of dirty, hard work, Jessie, to clean up some of the mess I made."

"Did you learn something from it?"

"Yep, cleaning up the soot that fall gave me a lot of time to think about building fires on tar roofs and letting anger get the best of me."

"Well, Sam, if you find yourself in a situation like the one that caused the fire, don't forget to use your deciphering mechanism. It has great potential for keeping us out of trouble," said Jessie.

"What on earth do you mean?" asked Sam.

"Our minds are magnificent. They are part of our internal compass—our wisdom. They have so much power over what we feel, think, and do. Our mind deciphers what we see around us—kind of like the navigator on an aircraft—and then we react to what we see or hear. That night, your radar picked up a threat—your perception of what the boys were saying. You deciphered it as making fun of you over a girl, and you became embarrassed and angry. Because of those emotions, you reacted quickly and it ended up creating the fire. How do you think you could have prevented the fire that night?" asked Jessie.

"I could have deciphered the boys teasing as just having fun and laughed it off. I could have just ignored them. Things would have turned out a lot better if I had," responded Sam.

"I've always thought you were a boy with keen insights, Sam! You are right. That would have helped." After a brief pause, Jessie said, "Now, tell me more about Holly."

That evening they stayed on the roof till the bats started swarming around the new lights looking for bugs. Jessie explained that he only used the warehouse to care for his birds—his man cave, he called it. "There is an easier way to get in, you know?"

"You mean the door?" teased Sam. "Do you own the warehouse too?"

"No, I just got permission from an old friend to use it," replied Jessie. "I prefer the open skies of the rooftop. It stirs the blood of my ancestors, and I feel the love of Mother Earth when the sun shines on my face. The air opens my mind and heart to Her messages and the openness of the sky gives me that sense of freedom every human strives to find. It also helps me stay centered on what is most important in life."

Sam shook his head as if agreeing; but then he said, "Jessie, I'd like you to help me make something special for Holly by using the feathers I have been collecting. I was thinking about a dreamcatcher."

"Of course, Sam, I'd love to help. Would Saturday or Sunday be better for you?" Jessie asked.

"Probably Saturday afternoon will work."

"Then Saturday it is at 1:00 PM!"

Before Saturday, Sam decided to ride his bike across the Suspension Bridge to the craft store on Elm Street to pick up a few supplies. As he approached the bridge, he remembered the day he crossed it to move to Kentucky. *I was so unhappy*, thought Sam. *But look what has happened because of that move.* Once he got to the store, he found some beads that he thought Holly would like and some pretty feathers that were turquoise blue.

Saturday couldn't come fast enough! Sam headed to the roof with all his supplies plus a chair. In his box of supplies was the shoebox full of his feathers with the lid tightly secured. He had not realized that he had collected so many feathers, and that didn't include the ones Joey had used for his artwork.

When Sam arrived, Jessie was already there with his bag of supplies. He had made a table for working on the project out of some boxes and an old board. Jessie had covered the makeshift table with a Native American blanket. It was all very cool to Sam. They laid out their tools, feathers, leather, and beads on the table.

Before they began their project, Sam turned to Jessie to say, "Jessie, the night I went back to the warehouse to get Marty, I had a very weird dream. After I woke up, I found a feather in my shoe. I've kept that feather as a reminder of how easy it is to do stupid things."

"Well, tell me about your dream."

Sam relayed the whole weird thing to Jessie and that he thought the firefighter with blue eyes was his dad. Sam concluded by saying, "When I saw his eyes, I knew it was my dad; and I felt overpowering shame about leaving Marty in the warehouse. I mean I left Marty 30 feet in the air in a cage, for gosh sakes. I should have been ashamed!"

"Well, we've already covered that. What's done is done. The important thing is to learn from your mistakes. I'm interested to know what kind of feather it was. Do you have it in your box?"

Sam pulled out the feather, and Jessie immediately recognized it as the feather of a red-tailed hawk. Jessie paused as he looked it over and then responded, "That is even more interesting, Sam. Red-tailed hawk feathers are given to those who feel insecure or abandoned — left alone. Sounds about right for that situation, wouldn't you say? I think that message was sent to you for a reason. What do you think that is?"

Sam took a deep breath and stared down at his tennis shoes for a while. Many people would have been uncomfortable with the silence, but Jessie just let it happen. He knew Sam was doing some serious thinking about his question.

Sam finally answered, "I think I need to find out what happened to my dad. There is no doubt I still need answers."

"I think so too; but for now, let's think about your dreamcatchers. Remember what I told you about the importance of feathers in Indian culture?" asked Jessie.

"Yes, they are symbols of strength, honor, kindness, trust, love, and other honorable things," replied Sam.

"Right, so they need to be used carefully on objects like dreamcatchers," said Jessie. "For example, when an Indian gives the gift of an Eagle feather, it symbolizes great strength, courage, leadership, and prestige. It is a high honor to receive one of those feathers.

"Once I promised you we'd go through your box of feathers, and I don't think we ever got around to that. And this is the perfect time."

Sam handed Jessie his shoebox. "As I look through your feathers, I see you have one from a bluebird, a crow, several from pigeons and doves, a falcon, and a red-tailed hawk. I'd like to know when and where you found them if you can remember," said Jessie.

"I found the bluebird feather outside my school on the first night I ever played basketball. I found it the night that I gave Alex the assist that enabled him to make our winning shot."

"Well, a bluebird feather symbolizes happiness and fulfillment. Do you think basketball has given you that?"

"Sure thing! Basketball changed a lot of things for me. I got better grades. I didn't get notes from the principal, and the bullying stopped. Or at least, I think it was basketball that changed that."

Jessie smiled because he knew that was about the time he had befriended Noah and his gang and redirected their energy in more positive ways.

Jessie went through the entire shoebox of feathers to pick out those that had significant meaning and discussed each one with Sam. He quizzed Sam about the very colorful turquoise ones he had purchased for Holly's dreamcatcher; and he smiled at Sam and said, "They will be a fancy addition to the dreamcatcher, which I'm sure Holly will like.

"Sam, as you were telling me the stories about how you found the feathers, it seemed to me that you found them at very special times in your life or connected to very special people. Would you agree?"

Sam thought a minute, agreed, and then named several influential people in his life. Jessie was one of them.

"Well, I'm honored that you have included me among those important people, Sam. I need to tell you that when I met you, you gave me a most valuable gift—the gift of purpose. Neahaw.[24] That's Shawnee for 'thank you.'

"Purpose helps us stay focused. Without it in our lives, we wander like a feather blowing in the wind. It is not healthy for mind, body, or spirit. You needed a friend; I needed one even more. Thank you for your gift of purpose.

"Once you asked me about the notes I sent on B-52's leg. It was a note to myself. I sent it every day."

"What did it say?" Sam asked eagerly.

"It said, 'Use your instruments wisely.' Remember the night you drank too much alcohol and the Indian story about the serpent?"

"How could I forget that, Jessie," Sam said with a woeful look on his face.

Jessie stifled a chuckle and continued, "I told you why I started coming to the rooftop; it was a bad time in my life. I sent the notes to myself on B-52's leg, and pretended they were from my wife, Charlotte. They were to remind me of my navigation instruments. Do you remember what I said they were?"

Sam thought and then answered, "I think they were courage and wisdom!"

"Right on! Over the time I have known you, I have tried to teach you to find and use your wisdom and courage. Your mind—your deciphering mechanism—helps you to interpret what is happening around you. It helps us know how to react. But we can't let our emotions interfere."

Jessie noticed that Sam was far more attentive to his lessons now. *The measure of a boy becoming a man*, Jessie thought.

After Jessie paused, Sam jumped up, ran around the table, and gave Jessie a hug, something he had not done often. Sam had always wondered if Jessie had any family. He certainly had never talked about them much. He knew he had been married. So, cautiously, Sam asked, "Jessie, did you ever have any kids?"

"No, Sam, I was never given that blessing."

It was obvious Jessie didn't want to have a conversation about that, so Sam returned to the task of making the dreamcatcher. "Where do we begin on the dreamcatcher," asked Sam.

After giving it some thought, Jessie said, "Now, here's an idea. Would you like to make two dreamcatchers—one for Holly and one for you to keep that would include some of these very special feathers?"

"That sounds like a great idea, especially since I've been having these mighty weird dreams!"

"Well, great, then let's get started!"[25] Jessie pulled out two red willow branches about six-feet long. He had soaked them so they would be bendable. He asked Sam to form the two circles with the branches. They decided on a size that would be slightly larger than the size of Jessie's hand. Jessie carefully snipped off both ends of the branches and asked Sam to twist the ends a bit around each other to give the circles strength. Sam followed Jessie's instruction to the letter.

Jessie next instructed Sam on how to weave the string around the hoop to create the dreamcatchers — *not an easy task*, thought Sam. They were looking almost complete! And then, they got to the fun part.

"Now, Sam, you should have 6-8 inches of string to tie 3 or 4 feathers which dangle from the center of the dreamcatcher. You need to decide which feathers you would like to use for Holly's dreamcatcher?"

"I'd like to use some of the turquoise ones I purchased for color, but I'd also like to add a couple from my collection."

"We need to make it pretty and something she might like. If I were you, I'd try to pick at least one special feather that you could tell her represented your friendship. And you made a wise choice going with turquoise feathers instead of pink! I think you said she didn't like pink things."

Sam chose to add some of the gray and white pigeon feathers to the turquoise ones for Holly's dreamcatcher. They added some matching beads of white, gray, dark turquoise, and red.

Jessie helped Sam secure the feathers and then said, "It turned out beautifully. I think she will think it is cool. I see you added a dove feather. You know that stands for love?"

"Oh, my gosh, Jessie!" Sam managed to blurt out given his rising embarrassment.

Jessie couldn't help but chuckle. "Okay, Sam. Then on to the dreamcatcher you are going to keep."

Sam laid out all the feathers that reminded him of special people or times in his life—Officer Epstein, Troy, Dave, Mom, Gram, and even Noah. He wanted to add all of them to his dreamcatcher. Jessie reminded Sam he'd have to be very thoughtful about how to add the feathers since his circle wasn't that large. Next, Jessie encouraged Sam to choose just a few feathers to attach to his own dreamcatcher.

Sam thought about it for a minute, and then he selected five feathers. He said, "Jessie, I am adding a pigeon feather to remind me of B-52 and that messengers come in many forms. It was B-52 that connected me to you, and many of the lessons I have learned.

"I am adding the bluebird feather to remind me that if I have enough grit, I can accomplish great things and have fun doing it! It will remind me of Coach Cady and all my basketball friends.

"I'm adding the dove feather to remind me to love others simply, without expectation or conditions—like Joey does.

"I'm adding the crow feather to remind me to use my wits. It will remind me of my wisdom and courage—navigation instruments that are there to help me every day. It will remind me of you—the one who has trained me to become a brave warrior—a wiser navigator—for myself, Joey and others. Neahaw." And then he added as a joke, "That's Shawnee for 'Thank you.'

As Sam picked up the red-tailed hawk feather, he paused like he was thinking really heard about what to say. Then he added, "And, finally, Jessie, I am adding this one to remind me that I belong; and that I have lots of people that I am connected to in very important ways.

Jessie was getting tired, and his love for this young man was creating a little discomfort in his heart. It was a feeling he had tried to avoid since his wife died but one that he was becoming more used to. He told Sam how much he liked his dreamcatcher and suggested they call it a day.

As he left the roof, Sam paused to say one more thing to Jessie, "And, unless I forget to say AGAIN, I am *really* sorry I burned down your shack!"

Jessie smiled and replied, "You weren't alone in the burning, but you were alone in the telling. That was an honorable thing to do, Sam."

They departed amidst the emotion of two friends saying goodbye, and Sam went on home to talk to his mother about the dreamcatchers he made and a lot of other very important things.

Chapter 17: The Shoebox Message

The following day after Sam and Jessie made the dreamcatchers, Sam had an almost "adult" conversation with his mom. It was the day Sam found out that his dad was in the ground troops that marched through the rice paddies of Vietnam, going from village to village. And sometimes he had to follow orders that were very hurtful to his heart. Sam's mom told Sam about the stories his dad would tell her when he came home on furlough. "I began to notice a far-away look in his eyes, Sam," his mom confided.

Sam's mother gave him a shoebox in which she had kept the letters from his dad, Corporal Samuel Elijah Jeffries. She explained that the contents of the box would be hard to see and the letters hard to read. She said he could either go through the box alone or with her. He chose to go through it alone in his bedroom.

Sam looked at the pictures first. There was a picture of his dad in his army uniform. Sam noticed the funny hat; but in this picture, it was on his head. Then, there were several pictures of his buddies in the service. And finally, there was a grave marker. Nothing elaborate; in fact, it was like all the thousands of other white markers lining the hills of Arlington Cemetery.

There were also some small pins that indicated his rank in the army and some of his personal possessions at the time of his death — a watch, a pocket knife, and a wallet full of baby pictures and one of his mom.

Then Sam got to the bundle of letters. When Sam opened the first letter, he immediately noticed a feather on the top of the page. Tears came to Sam's eyes. It looked like his dad had drawn it, maybe out of boredom, maybe as he was thinking about what to say, or maybe just to make the paper look like stationery.

It probably was the last letter his dad wrote. The letter was two pages long describing stuff that he had been doing. It was the words in the last paragraph that brought tears to Sam's eyes:

I long to be back home with you and the children. My heart burns for the dreadful things I have done.

"All I want to see is the face of my Sabbie and Jenna's beautiful eyes—Like mine, you always said. And I want to hold that baby, Little Joey. I guess he's almost walking by now. Gayle, you are the love of my life, and I am forever yours. Please kiss my babies for me and tell them daddy loves them."

All my love, Sammy

Before Sam returned the shoebox to his mother, he decided to put a feather from his collection in with the letters from his dad. When he was sifting through his feathers to find the right one, he found the note he had written to his dad, "Daddy, where are you? I could use your help." Sam thought about what Jessie had said about feeling abandoned by his dad — and angry because of it. *The content of this shoebox is the message I've been waiting for,* Sam thought. *It answers my question, "Where are you?"* He decided to put a gray and white pigeon feather in the box. And then he remembered his dream on the night his team left Marty in the dumbwaiter — the night he got the red-tailed hawk feather, and the night he dreamed about his dad. *A message from the other side? I wonder,* thought Sam. The thought gave him a cold chill.

After spending the time he needed with the shoebox, Sam rejoined his mother in the living room. They sat for quite some time not saying much. Then, Sam's mom told him about the soldiers who had arrived at the door with the news that Corporal Jeffries was dead. He was found dead after a fight in a bar in Saigon. There was nothing honorable about it. Sam's countenance fell; a knot swelled up in his throat. Sam felt like the falcon had him by the throat again. But, then, Sam calmed down a little. *Messengers,* Sam thought, *come in all shapes and sizes, carrying messages that are sometimes good and sometimes bad.*

"I always planned on telling you, Sabbie, when you were older and could understand the sacrifice young men and their families make for their country. Even though patriotism is an honorable thing, war hurts. Thank you for bringing it up. It was time for you to know the truth. Maybe I should have told you sooner."

Then all Sam could do was hold on to his mother in one of those moments when the man he was becoming suddenly became the little boy he was. Sam simply said, "Thank you, Mom."

Sam went to his room to get ready for basketball practice. He looked at his dreamcatcher and ran his fingers across the soft edge of the red-tailed hawk feather. He thought about how his father had died. Remembering Jessie's words, Sam thought, *I guess my dad just lost touch with his internal compass. He couldn't find his way back home.* Sam sat for a long while by himself thinking about the box, his dad, and all the years he had longed for these answers. Then Jessie's words about courage and life's struggles came back to him, "You have the courage to face them within you. Find it unless you want to continue to be a helpless pigeon in the falcon's mighty claws."

Chapter 18: The Dove Feather

Time slips by so quickly. Before Sam knew it, more than a decade had passed since he read the letters in the shoebox. Sam and Jessie spent as much time as they could after Sam graduated from high school and during college but the visits didn't happen often. It was Jessie who helped finance Sam's tuition and books, and Jessie was always in attendance for special events. He was present and proud when Sam graduated from college with honors.

Following college, Sam married Jane, a girl he had met in college and following his break-up with Holly. Sam and Jane married one month after graduation and began their family soon after he landed a job as a child therapist at a local pediatric hospital.

During the spring of his 30th year, Sam was invited to speak at a conference in California on adolescent psychological health. The nation had experienced a rise in the number of youth with behavioral health problems.

After the long flight to Los Angeles, Sam knew he'd have to hurry to make the dinner on time. As one of the main speakers at a pre-conference banquet on childhood psychology, he had to be on time. He only had about an hour to get to the hotel and get dressed before his ride to the banquet arrived.

In his hotel room, he hurriedly showered and dressed in his best suit. As he looked in the mirror to slick back his always unruly hair, he noticed a little grey popping out around the temples. He put the notes for his speech in the front pocket of his suit and took one last look-me-over in the long mirror that hung on the bathroom wall.

Satisfied with what he saw in the mirror, he picked up his briefcase and made his way to the front of the hotel to wait for his ride. Finally, a long black limousine pulled up; and a chauffeur jumped out of the car, ran toward the passenger side, and ushered Sam into the back seat.

As Sam slid across the limo's lush leather seats, the reality of the moment overwhelmed him. He would be speaking to hundreds of professionals from across the country who were gathered to learn how to address the changing behavioral health needs of children. He was to share his experiences working with adolescents with suicide ideation.

On the ride to the conference venue, Sam's thoughts began to churn up all sorts of self-doubt. To calm himself, he double-checked that his notes were still tucked away in his coat pocket. *How many people will be there? Is my research ready for this kind of scrutiny? Will there be lots of questions?* He closed his eyes and took a deep breath. *"Decipher!"* he commanded himself as he tried to stop the thoughts swirling in his head. The mesmerizing hum of the limo's engine seemed to help.

The event was held just a few minutes from his hotel, so he didn't have much time to feel nervous or calm down. When the limo arrived at the banquet hall, the chauffeur opened the door of the limousine again for him. As Sam emerged, he saw Charlie Voss, a leading researcher in the field, waiting for him. It was Charlie who had invited him to speak. They exchanged polite greetings and headed toward the dining room, mixing research talk with weather, flights, and expectations for the event.

The banquet hall was full of youthful faces — young men and women hoping to make their mark in the field of psychology. It was Easter weekend, so Sam had not expected this many people to be in attendance. The tables were gleaming with shiny glasses, silverware, and china plates. Fancy, colorful napkins, and unusual floral centerpieces gave the room a very elegant, yet festive, spring feel.

Once everyone was seated, the waiters started serving. Folded cloth linens were draped over one arm and they were wearing white gloves. Sam had never attended anything quite this lavish in all his years.

The waiters served several courses starting with a selection of wine and soup, then salad, and finally the entrée. The waiter sat the covered plate in front of Sam. As the waiter lifted the cover, he said, "Bon appétit!" Sam smiled at the waiter and then glanced toward his plate. Poised strategically on a bed of brown rice and garnished with a sprig or two of parsley was a very small fowl-like thing. He thought it looked kind of like a mini turkey on Thanksgiving Day. His countenance fell.

As he stared at the small bird, it prompted him to take a second look at the menu placard that was displayed in front of each place setting before eating it—if he was even going to eat it. The card listed all the courses and then he noticed the dinner entrée was indeed squab. He closed his eyes and gulped at the thought of eating a baby pigeon, even if it was considered a delicacy in many countries.

That's when his cell phone rang. Relieved to be avoiding what he thought would be a very unpleasant experience of eating squab or watching others eat it, he excused himself from the table to take the call.

As he walked from the room, he glanced at his phone again—it was his mother's phone number. He grew concerned about the reason she was calling.

"Hello," he answered with hesitation.

"Hi Sam, I'm sorry to bother you," his wife responded. Sam immediately questioned why his wife was calling him from his mother's phone number. He felt his chest grow tight. And then his wife said, "I have some bad news."

Sam's heart stopped momentarily as he listened quietly to her. Eventually, he finally managed to say, "I speak in 15 minutes and then I'll be on the next flight to Cincinnati." He took a minute to collect his thoughts before going back into the banquet hall. Squab was far from his mind. He was bewildered and overwhelmed—the signs of being grief-stricken. As he walked toward his table, he knew he had to collect these feelings and tuck them away in order to give his speech. He consciously gathered them up and stuffed them not-so-neatly into an imaginary box, and then placed the box on a shelf in his mind. *I'll deal with you later*, he thought. Just as he sat back down at the table, Charlie Voss announced his name.

The speech went as planned and the response from the audience was better than Sam had anticipated. When it was over, he rejoined Charlie at their table and leaned toward him to whisper that he needed to leave immediately due to a family emergency. Charlie offered condolences and then, wearily, Sam started his journey home.

At the airport, he only had to wait about an hour for a late-night flight back to Cincinnati. It was a relief to board the plane so quickly. The rush to the ticketing counter and to the gate kept his mind busy.

Given the long nighttime flight, Sam planned to sleep. He snuggled down into the first-class seat with a blanket and a pillow that had been provided by the flight attendant but those emotions he had stuffed in the box before he spoke began pounding against the box's lid. His thoughts would have no part of sleep. He kept ruminating over the events of the evening, the news from Cincinnati, and his regret about having to leave the conference before hearing the other speakers as they shared their work.

The bumpy ride from turbulence didn't help soothe him to sleep either. Not long after the plane departed the Los Angeles Airport (LAX), the pilot turned on the "Seatbelt" sign and announced over the loud speaker that they would be experiencing unexpected turbulence throughout the flight and gave the instruction for passengers to remain in their seats with belts buckled. At the mention of the word "turbulence," Sam's body immediately grew more tense, and he thought about the irony of that word considering what lay ahead of him back home.

As directed, Sam snapped his seat into the upright position and tugged on his seatbelt to make sure it was secure. Then, as a distraction, he picked up some magazines that were in the pocket of the seat in front of him. One was *Popular Science* dated February 2013.[26] He leafed through the pages and one article caught his attention: "How homing pigeons find their way home: A new theory explains why homing pigeons are so good at navigating back to their nests and why sometimes they are not." [4] *What the hell*, Sam thought half-chuckling! *Will pigeons ever leave me alone?*

It was almost 8:00 AM when the flight landed at the CVG airport just outside Erlanger. Sam caught a taxi and arrived in front of his mom's apartment about 8:30 AM. The feeling in his chest and throat grew tighter. He paid the driver and grabbed his bags. He knew this was not going to be easy.

After the taxi pulled away from the curb, Sam stood, once again, in front of the long, narrow tunnel that separated the two row houses. He couldn't help but remember the very first time he looked down its long narrow path. For a ten-year-old boy, it had looked miles long and to a very scary place—full of unknowns. And now, even through the eyes of a man, it looked long and scary—full of different unknowns and situations he'd rather avoid. As he began the long walk through the tunnel, the feelings he had once experienced there returned. He felt the high walls of the buildings surround him with only a thin slice of sky above him. It was especially enveloping in the early morning hours.

As he was climbing the three flights of stairs to his mom's apartment, his apprehension about knocking on her door grew with each step he took. He paused on the second floor, which gave him time to catch his breath and think. *Wait,* he thought, *this is Easter morning!*

He decided to find the second-floor window. Perhaps he was avoiding what lay ahead or perhaps it was to search for strength to face it. Regardless, he found himself just standing there peering out the window. His thoughts were interrupted by a familiar sound....it was a ball bouncing around on the roof, so he crawled through the window and crept toward the corner of the building that jutted out from the side of the building. Just as he approached the corner, a basketball rolled toward the roof's edge right in front of him. Not far behind was Dave, his childhood buddy.

As an adult Dave and Sam couldn't have been more different. Dave was blue-collar and Sam was three-piece suit but they had a comradery that began when they were ten and had withstood the years and distance that exists between East Covington and Ft. Mitchell.

Dave was a weekend biker and had assumed the stereotypical appearance of one. He had unruly, frizzy hair the color of cinnamon with a long scruffy beard to match. He usually controlled his hair with a bandana tied like a do-rag and topped with a black leather cap turned to the back. Blue jeans and a black leather vest over a white t-shirt were his go-to clothes. A long chain which connected the wallet in his back pocket to his front belt loop hung to his side—his signature look. Biker boots finished off his strong, burley biker appearance.

"Bro!" Sam yelled.

Dave turned toward Sam's voice and Sam threw the ball back toward the basketball goal and followed it. Under the slightly dilapidated basketball goal, Dave gave Sam a hearty hug and said, "Wassup, Sam" in the classic cool way that was uniquely Dave but, this time, with an empathetic tone. "Man, I was hoping I'd see you here. I heard about Joey."

"Yeah, I haven't seen my mom yet. I've been in California."

"I heard. That's why I'm here. Is she doing okay?"

"Jenn said she was taking it pretty hard," I said and looked toward the apartment above us.

"I wouldn't expect any less. Your mom was the 'real deal'. I mean, she loved all of us—even me. Well, hey, get up there. Tell them all I'm thinking about them and will see them at the funeral."

As Sam turned to walk toward the window, Dave said, "Hey, we need to get together soon. I have lots to tell you about the old gang."

"For sure, Dave! Once I get past the next few days, I'll call you."

"That would be great," said Dave. Despite his rough, burly looks, Dave still had his gentle, humble sprit that showed in the tone of his voice, the look on his face, and his demeanor.

"I will," and with that Sam turned to face the turbulence. As he crawled back through the window, he heard the ball bouncing again and it brought back so many fond memories of their days on the rooftop.

As Sam headed toward his mom's apartment, his apprehension grew with each step he took. It was the same apartment where Sam had grown up. He and Jenna had tried to get his mom to move from Lee Street, because she was having difficulty climbing the stairs. But she insisted on staying there. "Joey is used to the area and the community is used to Joey. It's best if we stay here for him," she always said.

More than a bit winded, Sam finally arrived on the third floor. His legs were feeling the burn of the long, steep climb. But nothing matched the grief that was welling up inside his throat. He twisted the doorknob and was surprised to find it unlocked. He stepped just inside the door and Jenna was already there, along with her two children and Gram. But Sam did not see his mother.

It was a somber moment, no doubt. He could tell everyone had been crying. "Where's mom?" Sam asked.

"She's in your old bedroom—Joey's room—lying down."

Sam's mind was filled with questions as he walked toward the bedroom. "How? Why? What do we need to do?" He slowly opened the door. He could tell she was sleeping so he just stood there for a minute looking at the small figure that was draped across the bed. Her white hair was brushing the top of her collar and falling gently across her cheek. He wanted to grab her and hold onto her, but he didn't want to wake her. He just stood there, trying desperately to stop the hurt in his throat; and then he quietly closed the door.

When he got back to the living room, he asked Jenna what happened, "Where did he get the candy?"

"Mom had prepared his Easter basket as usual, and he got into it early while mom was busy doing something in the kitchen."

"Well, how do you choke on a chocolate Easter egg?" Sam asked.

"I don't know, but he did," answered Jenna slightly irritated. "Mom was in the kitchen when he stumbled from his bedroom clutching his throat. She realized he was choking but couldn't figure out how to help him. He just died, Sam," Jenna said as her voice cracked and tears streamed from her eyes.

Sam dropped into a chair with his head in his hands. He quietly sobbed into his palms as he created the scene in his mind. His mother — alone — with her grown son — helpless — watching him choke to death.

At that moment, Sam's mom entered the room and came to sit on the arm of the chair where Sam was sitting. "Sabbie, oh Sabbie, Joey is gone."

Sam turned to his mom and grabbed onto her legs. "I'm so sorry, Mom!"

"You've done nothing to be sorry for, Sam," she insisted.

"I haven't been here in months! I should have been spending more time with him. I should have been helping you!"

"No need looking back, Sam. No need looking back," she responded as she stared off into space.

As they went about their day, Sam had difficulty trying to console his mom, Gram, and Jenna. He was only one breath away from breaking down himself. He thought this was one of the hardest things he had ever done.

Seeing that he and others were so upset, Sam's mom made hot chocolate for the kids and a pot of coffee for the adults. As she, Gram, Sam, and Jenna sat around the kitchen table, they began as a family to plan Joey's funeral.

After the funeral, the family went back to their apartment on Lee Street. Friends stopped by from time to time to offer their condolences and share food. Sam went into his old bedroom—now Joey's room. Joey had displayed some of his special belongings on the tall shelves that lined one wall. When Sam moved out, he told Joey he was old enough to reach them now and encouraged him to fill them with his favorite things. He had model airplanes, a Mickey Mouse bank, action figures, and many strange things Sam didn't quite understand. There were several toys that he had gotten over the years, and even rocks from someplace—not particularly pretty rocks but something Joey must have liked. And there was the white dove feather, the one Joey found. *It was the day I learned an important lesson about foolish obsessions. Joey would have been about eight. I asked him to keep it, and he did,* Sam thought. Sam smiled as he placed the feather back on the shelf.

Joey had grown to be a tall, very round 22-year-old young man. He worked part-time as a bagger and did other odd jobs at the corner market. The owner knew the family and offered Joey the job as a favor to Sam's grandmother.

Joey's spirit was gentle; his mind still operating at the age of an eight-year-old. "He is — was — a gentle giant," Sam heard his mom say. She had entered the room while Sam was looking over Joey's collection.

"Yes, he was," Sam replied and hugged his mom. She recognized that Sam needed some quiet time so she left the room without notice. Sam walked over to the window to look down on the rooftop below as he had done so many times long ago.

What young boy is finding his magic on the roof now? Sam thought. He paused there at the window to remember the day he first saw Jessie on the roof. The way the roof looked after the fire. And the day he yelled at Joey for interrupting his time with the bird at the window.

All the visitors had gone when Sam went back to the kitchen. Jenna was wrapping up food to take home. She told Sam that their mom would be staying with her for a few days. Sam helped them to the car and then went back to the apartment to lock up and gather some things. He welled up with tears once again as he turned off the lights throughout the apartment and left to return to his apartment in Clifton.

Before leaving the building, though, he stopped at the second-floor window. Remembering what Jessie used to say about the healing power of the open sky, he decided to return to the rooftop.

On the roof, Sam found nothing — no shack, no chairs, no basketball hoop — no young boy's footprints. He looked toward the big open sky. It was dusk and the sun was throwing a burnt orange hue across the horizon. With his face toward the heavens, he opened his arms as if begging for comfort.

As the sky grew dark, the street lights popped on as if touched by a sorcerer's wand. He noticed a slight breeze as it brushed across his face, and he remembered the breeze that had started the fire. *Was it the breeze or a thought that started that fire?* Sam wondered. He glanced toward his old bedroom window — Joey's room. There was a light on. He was puzzled by it. He was sure he had turned off all the lights and a bit annoyed that he would have to go back to turn off the one in Joey's room.

As he turned to go back up to the apartment, something on the roof where the shack used to be caught his attention. He walked over to get a closer look. It was a feather; Sam couldn't help but smile. *So many feathers over these years,* Sam thought. *Jessie used them to teach me so much,* as he remembered his days on the roof with him. Sam reached down and picked up the feather. He looked at it closely. It was snow white, shadowed only by the darkness. *It looks just like Joey's dove feather,* Sam thought as he looked toward Joey's room. As he stood there holding the feather, the light went off. It took his breath away. Sam shivered as he thought about this powerful message of love. He smiled and kissed the feather. "I love you too, Joey," whispered Sam as he stuck the feather in his shirt pocket.

Still sad, but more encouraged, Sam crawled through the second-floor window. Standing in the long hallway was Jessie. Sam had not seen him in over a year, and he seemed much smaller in size. Jessie hobbled toward Sam and when he reached him, he took his strong arms and wrapped them around Sam's shoulders.

"Oh Jessie, I am so glad to see you!"

"It is good to see you too, Ni-kwith-ehi — my son," replied Jessie. "I had to come when I heard about Joey."

And then Sam pulled out the feather from his pocket and they began a chat about Joey's dove feather and all the other feathers across time and what they had meant to both of them.

Chapter 19: The Falcon's Claws

Dave had endured a much harder life than Sam. He had grown up in foster care and had lived in three different homes. He went to the last one in third grade and, fortunately, was able to stay with that family throughout his middle and high school years. Sam and Jessie had often talked about Dave's quick wit and wondered if he had developed his humor as a way to mask the emptiness that surrounded his early life. Dave and his wife became foster parents and adopted two. They did not move away from East Covington.

Later that summer Dave and Sam decided to take a short weekend trip to catch up and do some fishing. They planned a trip to a nature preserve in Indiana. They met up on 4th street in Covington and began the 2-hour drive to their destination. Sam was chattering about whether the accommodations would be okay since they didn't know anything about the retreat. Dave, being far more laid back than Sam ever thought about being, reassured Sam that Alex, their mutual friend, said it was great.

Sam had loaded the address of the nature preserve into the GPS on the new black Outback wagon he had purchased in the spring. They were cruising along when Sam brought up their high school reunion that was planned for November.

"Are you going?" Sam asked.

"Hmmm, not sure."

"Why wouldn't you? Won't everyone be there?"

"Look at you, Sam. You are a psychologist, Alex is a lawyer, and many of the other people we graduated with have accomplished a lot in those fifteen years. What have I done?"

"Dave, you….." Sam had just started his retort when the lady in the dashboard interrupted him.

"Turn right at County Road 26," she said curtly so like third-grade children their attention snapped to her command. But a quick surveillance of the location caused them to question her instructions because all they could see were corn fields! But like preschool children, they continued to follow the sometimes frustrated voice of the woman in the dashboard.

"Dave, I haven't forgotten about that conversation we were having and I'll be coming back to it after we find this place," Sam said. Inwardly, he was glad for the interruption because he wanted to be very thoughtful about his response.

The road was narrow but blacktop so navigating it wasn't too difficult. But when the GPS told them to make another left turn, the road got curvy and more narrow. They went up and down the hills following the tree-lined road. Sometimes there was a house or barn. There was no doubt they were travelling into the back woods which caused both of them to get a little nervous.

They came to a rickety bridge at the bottom of a long, steep hill. It crossed over a stream that was runoff from the hills — not too deep but enough to warrant a bridge. This one had apparently been standing, without repair, for quite some time. After crossing the bridge, they climbed back up the steep hill on the other side. That's when the GPS told them their destination was on the left. Dave looked at Sam and Sam looked at Dave. All they could see were pine trees – lots of them lining a long driveway. Obediently, Sam turned.

When they emerged from the pine trees, they could see a lake with a log cabin nestled nearby. It was a beautiful July day and the setting was gorgeous — just as the retreat/nature reserve had described in the travel brochure. Sam's anxiety about the investment was relieved.

"Wow, that has aged well," Dave said as they approached the small log cabin. "I wonder if it really was built in the late 1800's as the brochure said."

"You got me," Sam replied. "I'm just hoping for some modern conveniences inside."

They were not disappointed. The owners had updated the inside with just enough amenities to make the guests stay comfortable but yet maintain the character of the original structure. It wasn't large by any means – more like an oversized hotel suite.

They unpacked their bags and tucked enough clothes in the armoire for their three-day stay. The armoire was antique with its original finish; clean with no scratches or scrapes. It caused Sam to pause and marvel at the way the owners had managed to mix in fine old antiques into the slightly modern décor. *Something for everyone,* Sam thought.

It was late afternoon before they got the chance to explore what was outside the cabin. The brochure instructed them to leave through the back door and find the walking trail that would take them through the pines to a spot on the other side of the lake.

As instructed, they followed the trail till they saw two Adirondack chairs sitting on a platform near the lake. They decided to stop there and enjoy the late afternoon sun.

The view was spectacular! The cabin was nestled in the center of a pine grove. From this perspective, the lake looked like it was in the front yard of the cabin. The pines were mature with lofty, verdant boughs that created a canopy for picnic tables, flower pots, and a barbecue pit. A boat was leaning against one of the trees near the water's edge.

The lake had a blue tint and was sparking from the glow of the afternoon soon. A soft breeze created sun reflective ripples that really magnified its beauty. Martins were perched on their small house that had been erected near the water's edge as a sanctuary for them.

"I can't think of a better way to spend a day," Sam said to Dave as they looked over the lake.

"Beats seeing the dentist," Dave responded in his usual quick wit. "I was supposed to be there today."

Sam hadn't known Dave cancelled a dental appointment so he turned to him and quizzed, "Did you get your appointment rescheduled?"

"Nah, my teeth will still be there next week."

Oh, Dave, will you ever change, Sam thought.

Just at that moment a falcon bolted from the sky and snatched a bird that was sitting on top of the martin house. In a burst of activity, the martin house seemed to shake as the other birds took flight. "What's up with that shit!," shouted Dave as he jumped up from his chair. He had the burley look but he was a city boy through and through. It rocked the tranquil scene for sure, but Sam had seen it before so it was not as impressive to him as it was for Dave.

Sam reminded Dave about the time Jessie had entrusted the pigeons' care to him because Jessie was going to be gone for quite some time. "One night as the pigeons were coming home to roost, a falcon swooped down and grabbed one of the pigeons in midair — right in front of my eyes! Don't you remember that?"

"Yeah, kinda."

Sam resumed his tale, "The falcon held the pigeon with its powerful claws and flew away. Shocked, I just stood there watching the mighty bird become nothing but a speck in the sky. When I finally got the chance to tell Jessie about it, he used it as a chance to teach me about the power of negativity. He said 'Negative thoughts that get stalled in our minds and hearts are like the falcon's mighty claws. Thoughts elicit emotions. If you don't resolve the negativity, it will grab you around the throat and carry you off.'

"Dude, I get that but, if you don't mind, I'm heading back to the cabin now."

As Sam walked behind Dave, he kept thinking about how fast and suddenly it all happened. Even though Sam had seen it before, this time, it was with a new perspective – through the eyes of an adult and not a child. The bird had flown with astonishing speed down near the water's edge and with its large fierce claws grabbed the martin as he, too, was sunning himself on top of his sanctuary.

"Dave, seeing the falcon again reminds me of my friend Amelia's untimely cancer diagnosis. Amelia is a nurse practitioner at my hospital. The therapists in my office often work with Amelia for mutual patients. She was 32 and two months pregnant when she got the diagnosis — ovarian cancer on the cusp between stage 3 and 4. Never in my life have I ever seen a human come so close to death and not die as I did with Amelia. She had always demonstrated positive character traits — honesty, fairness, forgiveness, humor — but when I observed her courage through the ordeal of her ovarian cancer, I was totally and humbly impressed," Sam went on.

"Like that fast-moving falcon, the diagnosis hit her — hit us all really. She was pregnant on Friday, lost the baby on Saturday, and having major surgery on Monday. The prognosis was grim — women with stage 4 have poor outcomes. When the office staff heard the diagnosis, we were scared, very scared. We all knew what Stage 4 meant," Sam continued.

"Following radical surgery, she was scheduled for 14 weeks of heavy-duty chemotherapy. Over the course of her treatment, we took turns taking her to her appointments, food to her home, landscaped her yard, and fed her dogs. I even volunteered to shave my head."

Dave jumped in, "Well, that would have been a sight!," – again trying with his humor to offset the heavy emotion attached to this story.

Sam returned to his story, "On one occasion, I remember leaving thinking I would never see her alive again. Yet, through it all Amelia remained courageous, positive, and with an unrelenting determination to beat it."

In one of the most amazing moments in Sam's relationship with Dave, Dave responded to Amelia's story, "That's remarkable, Sam. Through my own experience in foster care, I had to find the strength and courage to fight the falcons around me. Grit rises up from a hunger to survive."

"You are so right, Dave! It's that combination of courage and grit that enables not only to survive but also to bounce back. The falcon had Amelia by the throat but she fought back—hard! She did it through positive thinking—by controlling the thoughts that caused her to fear the future, by pushing them out of her head and replacing them with thoughts about returning to work, being cancer free in 5 years, and surviving to age 50."

As their conversation waned, Dave continued toward the cabin, but Sam stayed down by the water's edge for a awhile, still thinking about the analogy of the falcon. When Sam finally got back to the cabin, Dave was sitting at the small table in the kitchen. He had a Mountain Dew in front of him—his go-to drink.

"Man, did that falcon scare you that much?" I asked.

"It's just creepy, and the fate of the martin reminded me of every kid I've ever encountered in the foster care system." His response caused me to pause and reflect on the wisdom behind his words.

We spent the evening in front of a fire talking about old times, new 2 new kids in his care, and falcons. And before we went to bed I said to Dave, "Please don't ever underestimate what you have accomplished. You have climbed up from immeasurable challenges. You are resilient and wise. Now, you are helping children do the same. That is noteworthy and an accomplishment that not many can be proud of!"

Chapter 20: Noah Couldn't Escape

Dave ran into Noah at the medical center in late August and asked if Dave could arrange a time for the two of them to meet with Sam. When he got home, Dave called Sam to tell him about Noah and his desire to meet up at the basketball courts in Mainstrasse. "How about Saturday morning," Dave concluded. They hadn't played basketball since high school, except for those few hoops they shot the day Sam came home from California. Sam agreed but questioned, *But why Mainstrasse?*

On Saturday morning Sam searched his garage for a basketball that had enough air in it to bounce and headed to the park. At 9:00 AM on a Saturday morning in August, there aren't too many kids playing in the park so it was a good time for two older dudes to meet up.

When Sam arrived, he saw Dave sitting on the bench with another man. As he approached them, he realized it was Noah. He had not seen Noah in ten years or so and had he not been sitting with Dave, he probably would not have recognized him at all.

When Sam looked at Noah on the bench, his short-sleeved shirt hung over a carcass like it would hang on a chair. Skin drooped on the thin arms jutting out below the sleeve of his shirt. His face had little color; his eyes sunk into prominent cheek bones. He was just a faded remnant of the boy Sam grew up with—his nemesis in grade school who turned out to be something of a friend in high school.

Like a snowflake's fall to earth,[27] Noah's journey was full of adverse atmospheric conditions. In his east Covington neighborhood, it was hard to hide family business — everyone knew when the police car or ambulance showed up at your house or a distant relative came to visit.

So everyone knew, you see, that Noah's dad liked his alcohol and it made him do stupid things, embarrassing things. His dad spent more time in jail than out; and, despite it all, Noah loved his dad.

Noah's dad also had a tendency toward violence and he took it out on his mom — often. Being the oldest of his three siblings, Noah tried to protect his mom and his younger brothers when his Dad was on one of his binges. And that's when his dad took his anger out on Noah. Despite it all, Noah loved his dad.

Little did Sam know when he was ten, the reason why Noah was being a bully to him. You see, the falcon started circling Noah when he was young and Noah was just emulating it's taunting behavior.

Noah's experiences were not unique. Nearly one in eight children have three or more negative life experiences associated with levels of stress that can harm their health and development.[28] As a therapist, Sam saw these children every day in his work.

Children like Noah live in chronic, toxic stress. It's like God knew we might encounter bears or other threats so he included adrenaline, glucose, and cortisol in our bodies to help us fight or run from any threat we might encounter. When Noah's dad came home in a rage, Noah's heart would beat faster, his breathing would speed up, his senses were sharpened, and glucose and other nutrients flooded his bloodstream. He was ready to take on his Dad, if needed.

All of us experience this stress response most days. Our adrenaline goes up, we respond, and we bring it back to normal — homeostasis or balance. For children like Noah who live with multiple, chronic and/or severe adversities, their body seldom applies the brakes. Their emotional turbulence — fear, insecurity, tension, anxiety, and threat — keeps their body's survival mechanism activated.

Without de-escalation, the hormonally-propelled stress response can impair the way young brains develop, and negatively impact their immune status, metabolic systems, and cardiovascular function over time.[29]

The falcon finally snatched Noah by the throat and started carrying him off when Noah was in the sixth grade. He raced home from school, into the house, and found his dad hanging from a beam in the garage. That catastrophic event tore him apart, because, despite it all, Noah loved his dad.

Noah had the aptitude to be successful in school and in life — his teachers saw that and tried to help, but Noah needed more than what the teachers could give. His brain circuits had been rewired — redirected — in ways to help him interpret and deal with the severity of his toxic stress. And it left him in psychological and emotional turmoil.

Like other children living in toxic environments, Noah picked up some bad habits to help him ease the mental and emotional pain associated with toxic stress. For children and youth, it might look like pulling their hair out strand by strand—nothing too noticeable—until one day there is a bald patch in their crown. For Noah, it was the experimentation with cigarettes, alcohol, and pot.

For other children, it might be engaging in promiscuous sexual behavior; or it might be deciding to puke up food to maintain a lower body weight; or it might be cutting themselves to take control of the pain; or it might be taking dangerous risks with climbing, cycling, or driving. For adults, it can mean more of the same. If these behaviors continue over time, it can lead to serious legal and social consequences as it did in Noah's life.

People in the community knew Noah's substance use had escalated over time and by the time he was twenty-five, he had lost any job he was able to get, was addicted, and was arrested for petty theft.

Noah's story reflects the devastating impact of chronic childhood adversity. It might be never having enough to eat; or being bullied for being different; or being insulted, blamed, ridiculed by a parent, other caregiver, teacher, or coach time after time. Frequent yelling of instructions, bellowing of commands, or screaming of reprimands can cause a young child to cower in the stairwell, behind a chair, or under their bed—either literally or figuratively.

As chronic and/or severe experiences mount up, the likelihood of a negative life trajectory increases. For Noah, he tried on multiple occasions to stop using drugs; he even got his GED in prison and got accepted into a local college. Without fail, his symptoms of addiction would recur. He dropped out of college and returned to his old ways including more serious crime that got him arrested and back in prison for a few years.

He did have several small wins along the way that eventually got him to where he is today. His disease of addiction is managed, but he struggles with the lasting consequences of early decisions — poor health and lack of direction or purpose.

"Hey, Noah, it's good to see you," Sam said as he approached. "You too, Dave," Sam added as he jabbed at his arm. Sam decided not to take a jab at Noah's bony arm.

"Hi, Sam, how are you doing?" Noah asked.

"Trying to keep up with work, a wife, and a kid!" Sam replied. "And you?"

Sam knew the question would lead us into a conversation about his illness and he let it. Noah wanting to meet was a clue.

"I'm sure sorry to hear about the liver disease, Noah. Is there anything I can do?"

"Only if you have two livers!" he replied.

Dave piped in – "I thought we had two."

"Uh NO, Dave, - that's kidneys!" Noah scoffed but added a smile.

Despite meeting under the cloud of Noah's serious illness, that Saturday morning the three of them shot the ball at a hoop till someone yelled, HORSE just as they had done when they were kids. It didn't take long for Noah to get winded so he tossed the ball to Sam and said, "I hope you have a short memory Sam."

Noah could see the puzzled look on Sam's face as he caught the ball.…then, in a kind of make-amends way, Noah said "I wasn't very kind to you, Sam, when we were young. I mean. I'm sorry, really sorry." Then he turned and weakly walked away leaving Sam standing there like a dumbfounded 10 year old.

Awkwardly, Sam yelled to him, "Till next time, Noah," but in his heart Sam questioned whether there would be a next time.

Noah raised his hand over his head in acknowledgement as he continued to walk away.

Chapter 21: Alex's Bully Within

After settling the legal affairs surrounding Joey's death, Sam reached out to Alex who was now a lawyer in a Covington law firm. Even though they had both still lived in the East Covington neighborhood during college, they lost touch after high school. Alex was attending law school in Northern Kentucky and Sam was across the river studying psychology.

Alex's family had moved to Covington when he was 10 from a small town south of Covington. It was Dave who introduced him to Sam because he needed more players for his basketball team. As it turned out, Alex and Sam were more athletic than Dave and the two of them ended up playing four years on the junior and varsity high school teams together. Unfortunately, their lives went in separate directions upon graduation.

Sam called Alex's law firm and asked for an appointment. They decided to meet over coffee at a little place off Greenup Street. Like comrades of old, they embraced upon sight and settled in for a business meeting mixed with remembrances and banter.

"You have done well, Alex," Sam started off.

"Who would've thought it, right?" Alex responded. And immediately Sam was reminded of something Alex had shared during a leadership development retreat when they were seniors in high school. They were asked to identify challenges or barriers to achieving their goals. Alex floored his small group and the leader by telling them about his self-doubt that caused him to question every decision, every action, every relationship.

Alex was the youngest of four siblings. His father was not an alcoholic but he would binge drink when he had the money, along with Alex's grandfather and uncles too. There were frequent fights, lots of yelling, and threats to hurt either themselves or others—including those between his mother and father. And the whole town knew it.

To compound the chronic tension from the alcohol abuse, his mother got cancer when he was 6 and was physically and emotionally absent for almost two years. Had it not been for extended family, he would never have gotten a bath, had clean clothes, or any sense of security.

Alex's challenge was embedded in a culture of "haves" and "have nots" in the small rural town where his family had lived in Central Kentucky before moving to Covington. Growing up as the son of a tenant farmer and town drunk made him a "have not." Whether real or imagined, as a child in that environment, self-doubt and imperfection began to take root; and, once rooted, self-doubt is hard to extinguish.

"You have done well, Alex," Sam insisted. "We both have."

"Thank you Sam. It is so good to see you. I heard about Joey and I am so sorry that his life ended so tragically."

"It's getting easier, but his death is why I need to talk to you. My mom……" and on their conversation droned till their coffee consumption dictated a trip to the men's room for both of them.

As Sam walked to his car after the meeting, he thought about the bully in Alex that would not leave him alone. Even as an accomplished lawyer, he still questioned himself. *Like Dave, Sam thought. How do we ever overcome the entrapments of our childhood?*

It got Sam to thinking about self-doubt and how it impacts his friends, himself, and his patients. When he got back to the office, he decided to jot down a few notes on the topic that might help him help others.

- "It's in all of us, some more than others—that threatening 'anti-self' that distorts the very sense of who we are.[30]
- The "anti-self" has been called an internal enemy that seeks to derail us, cause us to question our abilities, and think of ourselves in negative ways. Jessie would have called it a falcon with mighty claws.
- As we grow, we develop a sense of self that is clouded by reality (who we really are) and fantasy (who we would like to be). But the parasite—that bully within—butts in with constant chatter, mixed messages—always coaching us to stick with our ego defenses. This is the essence of self-doubt.
- As we interact with others each day and navigate decisions that need to be made or actions that need to be taken, our "selves" fight for our attention. The anti-self often wins.
- You see, the scars of Alex's childhood were NOT from being abused; they were much deeper—embedded in a culture of comparison and always coming up short.

- Child logic emanates from entrenched inner pain—fear, anxiety, shame, hopelessness, and powerlessness—that influences how we think and act. Child logic is laden with misunderstood emotion from previous experiences.[31]

Then Sam started thinking about ways to help Alex and Dave overcome the challenges of self-doubt.

- "There comes a time when adults should be able to recognize our child logic and its source—the interactions with the many people of our past.
- Interactions can be those we've been a part of or those that we have observed. Those early interactions with the people in our lives either taught us lessons in love, made us feel the bitterness of their own self-doubt, or did both.[32]
- These interactions form memories that we file away in our brain and that continue to play a role in shaping our outlook on life, our resilience, our character, and our behavior.
- As a child and adolescent, we learn the "rules of the game" by watching adults around us. We reflect the strengths and weaknesses we see in them. We are obsessed with our need for their approval; and that need persists into adulthood. We continue to judge our own actions by others' reactions and measure our own abilities by their judgements.

- Like Alex, in time, we all need to acknowledge that our childhood was not perfect and that many of our choices may not have been the best. We need to learn to grow from them and move on. We need to see ourselves as imperfect humans like all the other imperfect humans on the planet—with strengths and limitations. And that's okay."

Sam put down his pencil and shook his head with dismay at the intrusive bully that lies deep within all of us.

Chapter 22: Feathers Across Time

In September, Sam called Jessie to ask if he could stop by. There was no answer. He called the second day, still no answer. And the third day, no answer. That's when Sam went to Holman Street. As he was standing on the front porch, Jessie's neighbor came over to tell Sam that yesterday an ambulance had taken Jessie to the hospital. Sam went directly to the large, aging building just off Madison Avenue and asked the lady at the information desk where he could find him.

She looked at a computer screen and asked for Sam's name. "Aw," she said, "he has you listed as next of kin. Mr. Walters is in Room 216, cardiac ICU." He thanked her and headed toward the elevator and questioning why Jessie had listed him as his next of kin.

When Sam got to the unit, it seemed locked down only allowing certain people in. He told the receptionist sitting near the closed doors that he wanted to visit Room 216. She asked his name and again checked a computer. Then, in a grave tone, she asked if he would wait till she checked with the nurse. That's when Sam began to think Jessie's condition must be critical. He took a deep breath.

The nurse returned from the unit and told Sam that he could only see Jessie for 10 minutes. He thanked her and hurried to Room 216. Upon arrival, he gingerly cracked the door to see what awaited him on the inside. Suddenly, the memory of the first day he snuck onto the roof and peeked inside Jessie's old shack popped into his head. And with the memory came a feeling of strong admiration intertwined with love and remorse. Sam had let far too many months go by without seeing Jessie, attending to him. It was rekindling the guilt surrounding Joey's death. We do that as adults. We get so wrapped up in our daily lives that we forget to nurture those relationships that are important to us.

Jessie's frail body looked small on the bed. Sam remembered when he first met Jessie; he thought he was the biggest person he had ever seen. And Jessie was, actually, about 6'2" with broad shoulders and a waist that matched. But that was in the mid 80's and Jessie was in his 50's. The man on the bed bore little resemblance until he opened his eyes.

Weakly, Jessie raised his arm in a greeting. Sam grabbed it and held it tight. "Sab," Jessie said. *My gosh he hasn't called me that in years*, Sam thought. "I'm glad you are here." And then for the short ten minutes remaining, Jessie tried to tell Sam what to do when he passed away.

When he started, Sam interrupted him, "Jess, we can talk about all that later." Sam's rational mind could see that there was not much time but his heart was screaming 'you can't die!'

"Sam, my spirit is slipping away and I want you to know what to do." About that time, the nurse came into the room to check vitals and, Sam thought, as a not-so-obvious reminder of his being over the ten-minute limit.

"I'll stay close-by," Sam said to both of them as he exited the room. He had a lot of time to think during that hour sitting in the ICU waiting room. *How do you let go of that someone who has been such an important part of you?* He thought. He could feel a corner of his own heart dying with him. *Is this what my patients mean about that hole in their heart*, he wondered.

Per Jessie's instructions and following the call from the hospital, Sam went to Jessie's home on Holman street. It was one of the smallest row houses on the street with only one floor, one room wide, and three rooms deep. It was a familiar place; Sam had been there many times so he knew just where to look for the envelope labeled "advance directives." It was in the long middle drawer of the 1950's desk that sat in the corner of the living room.

Sam opened the envelope; there were several things. The first document was the living will — what to do if he became a vegetable. *Thankfully, I didn't have to use this*, Sam thought. The second document had contact information for his lawyer who would help settle his estate and other important numbers of people to call. Sam turned his attention to the third document. It was held together with a thick, red rubber band, handwritten, and titled, "Feathers Across Time."

Sam laid the other documents aside. He didn't need the advance directives and he thought, *I will contact the lawyer tomorrow*. His eyes were drawn to the papers secured by the thick rubber band. He removed the binding and turned to the first page. It was a kind of diary.

July 1975 – I found a scrawny kid in my shack today. I don't know if he was rummaging through my things or not. He said he lives in one of the apartments in the building and is not one of the boys that keeps bothering the pigeons. I startled him when I opened the door of the shack and he scampered past me as I stood in the doorway. I think I might of scared him.

No shit, Sam thought with a smile about the memory.

August 1975 – his name is Sam but his family calls him Sab or Sabbie. I guess B-52 has been pestering him every morning. He came back with his mother today. I actually knew her when she was in the elementary school where I worked. And I remember her late husband – Sam's Dad. He was one of the boys from the neighborhood that were killed during the Vietnam War. He was a rounder in high school; I thought the Army might do him some good.

He never told me that! Sam thought. *Hmmm…..*

September 1975 - Sam is interested in the pigeons and he says he's starting to collect feathers. He asked about my Native American roots so I told him how Native Americans use feathers as symbols of strength, honor, kindness, trust, love, and other honorable things. And that when we find them, they can be a message from "the other side."

I hope so, Sam thought.

October 1975 – Sam is here often and he has hundreds of questions about the dreamcatcher on the wall, the navigation magazines in the shack, and, of course, about pigeons. I enjoy his visits.

I hope so, Sam thought.

November 1975 –The injury I received in 1944 is flaring up. The nerve damage is causing more pain than I can stand most days. The docs at the VA say I need to have surgery if I want to continue to live a normal life. I have to do it or I won't be able to continue going to the roof to work with the pigeons – and Sam. I can see Sam's hurt. His mom has not told him the whole story about his dad and its placed a ball of anger in the pit of his stomach.

Sam felt tears creeping into his eyes.

January 1976 –I haven't seen Sam in several months. I hope he's okay. My leg is healing from the surgery. I'm able to move around the house without much difficulty. As soon as the weather gets warmer, I think I'll walk over to Lee Street.

April 1976—Got a note from Sam on the bottom of B-52's foot. He's such a clever boy! He says they're gonna hurt the birds. I think I need to see Sam.

June 1976 – Some guy named Noah is bullying Sam. He is also one of the kids that has been harassing the pigeons. I tried to teach Sam some ways to deal with Noah and the other bullies. I told him about Bottleneck, the name some boys had given me when I was a kid. I don't think it helped.

August 1976 – A falcon got one of the pigeons today. I hated to hear it but Sam hated it even more. Poor kid. I tried to teach him that day about how quickly changes can happen in our life and how better to face them.

"Seriously – the best lesson you ever taught me Jessie," Sam said out loud but it was only a whisper.

July 1979 – I can't believe it! Sam and his buddies caught the roof on fire. Insurance will take care of the damage but Sam has to face the consequences of his irresponsibility. I am proud that he owned up to it. That took a great amount of courage. Maybe some things I 've tried to teach him has stuck.

On it went – page after page - year after year of memories about their encounters, Jessies thoughts, and his hopes for me. Sam continued to scan the pages till he came to the post about the day they made the dreamcatchers.

May 1983- We made dreamcatchers today using the feathers Sam has collected since he moved to Covington. It is quite profound how those feathers really told a story of his life. He used each one to make his dreamcatcher—the one he would keep—the one signifying those special people in his life. As a senior in high school, I think it helped him reflect on the good things that had happened in his life.

Sam selected four feathers to add to the dreamcatcher. He had several from B-52. She was already gone so when he added one to remember her, it warmed my heart. He said he was adding B-52's feather because she was the one who connected us. That bird was so special!

Then he almost made me cry when he added a red-tailed hawk feather—symbolic of belonging—to remind him of our friendship—of me.   When he added the feather, he said that I, like a father, had helped him develop courage and wisdom to find his own path.

I praised him for his thoughtful choice of feathers and thanked him for including me. And then, I suggested he really needed to talk to his mom about his dad. He did that later the same day.

Sam's eyes had filled with tears. He looked around the room for a box of tissues. The room was full of Jessie's familiar things—his dreamcatcher, pictures, books. Things Sam had made in school and given to him. But there were no tissues.

Sam walked into Jessie's bedroom. His bed was made, his slippers beside the bed. No tissues. Sam continued his search into the bathroom. There he found his bottles of medicine, his shaver beside an old mug and shaving brush Sam had given him long ago, and he also found tissues. By this time, Sam was much in need.

When Sam got back to the living room, he put the rubber band back around the pages and tucked them under my arm to take home to read completely. *I will tell Jessie's story to my kids one day*, Sam thought as he closed the door of Jessie's home.

Chapter 23: Life's Not-So-Little Gifts

Per his instructions, Jessie's body was cremated. Sam had his ashes sitting in an urn on a shelf in his home office. Jessie had left specific instructions on how to release them in the last entry in his diary dated May 22nd, 1999.

Sam, I'm sitting here at my kitchen table at 7:30 in the morning. Steam is rising from my cup of coffee like a clue or warning given by our Creator to keep us from burning our lips. One of life's little gifts—often overlooked or acknowledged. Life's gifts come in all sizes, shapes, and life forms. This old Indian who talks to birds has been blessed with many gifts—none more present or beloved than you. Each time you start the morning and see the steam rising from your coffee or tea, remember the gifts we have all around us. Remember me and smile.

Now, when my time has come, I want you to walk across the Suspension Bridge from North to South scattering my ashes into the Ohio River. As my ancestors did long ago, I will walk the banks of the River till I find my new home.

In late September, Sam called Dave to ask him to go with him to spread the ashes. Dave agreed. When Dave picked Sam up, he had two little boys in the back seat—about 5 and 8.

"Who are these guys?" Sam asked.

"It's Tommy and Brian. They are living with me now."

"Well, it's very nice to meet you guys," Sam said. They smiled and bowed their heads. *Shy,* Sam thought but his focus was on the task at hand.

Dave drove the car across the Suspension Bridge and they parked on Pete Rose Way. When they emerged from the car, Sam noticed the warmth of the Sun on his face and he heard the sound of a large barge moving down river. He was glad they had picked such a nice day. Dave suggested that they stop when they approached the Bridge to say a few words.

"Okay. That would be nice. Do you want to go first?" Sam asked.

"No, dude, I think this is your honor," Dave replied.

The closer they got to the bridge, Sam could hear the sound of a large barge travelling down river. He was carrying the urn and Dave and the boys were following behind.

When they arrived at the Bridge, Sam was still clutching the urn. They stood there for a few minutes — for the boys it seemed longer. Thoughts were swirling in his head as to what to say. How do you capture the essence of a relationship as important as his and Jessie's in a few words?

Sam reached his hand into the jar and grabbed a handful of ashes. They were soft to the touch. Then he turned to Dave and the boys and said, "This was my friend Jessie. He was of the Shawnee Tribe that settled in Ohio long ago. I met him when I was only a little older than you, Tommy. What we are doing today is to honor him and his people."

As they walked, Sam released the ashes into the air letting them fall across the water. Sam continued, "Boys, the day I crossed this bridge coming into Covington to live, I was so mad about moving and having to go to a new school. As it turned out, if we had not moved, I would never have met Jessie or Dave." This ceremonial service was to honor Jessie, but for Sam it was the beginning of another journey, one that he had not yet realized he was destined to take.

When they got to the middle of the Bridge Sam stopped and turned to Dave and the boys and said, "Every human begins life's journey connected to another human, their mother. That connection embeds a need for human relationships deep within our being. Over time, those relationships become anchors or strong supports that keep us centered and focused. There is no doubt that Jessie anchored me. He taught me truth and courage, the power of love and forgiveness. He strengthened me with his caring and kindness. He understood me when I couldn't understand myself. He was my guide when I couldn't find my way. I thrived because of it."

Sam's words began to crackle in his throat, so he stopped. There was a long pause and Dave sensing Sam needed help added, "Jessie had a positive influence on many of us. Remember Noah and, for that matter, me. Remember the time when we were playing basketball in junior high. He knew I wasn't going to have anyone there for me on parent night, so he came for me. He stood up when the announcer called my name and held up my jersey. He also taught us lots of stuff, you more than me, Sam, but it also rubbed off on me." Then Dave paused and turned to the boys who were walking a step behind, but listening attentively, "Tommy and Brian, your parents were taken too soon in your young life. I promise I will do my best to be that anchor for you."

Sam had regained his composure so he added, "Okay, here's to Jessie and all the other Jessies in the world who can reach beyond themselves to better the life of those around them. Thank you, Jessie, for being my—I mean our—friend, one of our most precious gifts." He paused again and earnestly said, "Neehaw." And recognizing the boys needed an interpretation, he said, "Neehaw is Shawnee for thank you." And the boys repeated it in unison, "Neehaw."

And with that they all took some ashes from the jar— even the little boys. While they continued their path across the Bridge to the South Bank, Sam heard Dave and the boys saying, "To Jessie" as they slowly released their ashes. It warmed Sam's heart.

When they got to the other side, Sam thanked the boys and Dave for helping him honor Jessie by releasing his ashes into the air, water, and earth—"fitting for a Native American," Dave said. Since they had to walk back to the car, the boys scampered ahead of Sam and Dave on the Bridge. The boys seemed enthralled by the majestic structure. They would pause occasionally to watch the boats on the water and to observe the Covington and Cincinnati skylines. Sam heard Tommy, the youngest, say, "Hear that? It's the Bridge singing a farewell song to Jessie."

"That's a gentle soul," Sam said to Dave.

"He truly is, Sam. One of the best kids we've ever had."

Our walk gave Dave time to tell Sam the boys story. They were brothers whose parents had been killed in a fiery crash caused by a drunk driver. The agency had been able to find homes for each of the boys, but they hoped they would find one family who would take them both in order to keep them together. And, of course, Dave took them in.

"It was a very good day," Sam said to Dave as he pulled up in front of Sam's Ft. Mitchell home. They said their good-byes and Sam gave the boys a high-five.

Sam carried the empty urn back in the house and placed it back on the shelf alongside the red-tailed hawk feather. Before leaving the urn, he looked inside. A few remaining ashes were nestled in the bottom of the urn. Sam was glad to this remnant of his lifelong anchor still with him.

Chapter 24: The Reunion

November came and so did Sam and Dave's 15-year high school reunion. Sam had talked Dave into going so they decided to go together. Like high-school kids before a prom they had discussed what they should wear, what they should drive, and should they go alone or with their wives. They decided to wear casual slacks and a sweater, drive Sam's Outback wagon, and not take their wives. But, they did decide to call Noah to see if they could pick him up.

"No, dudes, those people don't want to see me," Noah replied, when Dave called him. But Dave wasn't having any part of it.

"Noah, it's very casual. You can just wear what you've got. We're not dressing up. We'll pick you up at 7:00 pm."

And that's what they did. Right on time. They stopped at Noah's place in Ludlow to take him to the Gardens, a reception hall in Park Hills. Dave and Sam didn't even give it a thought what Noah would wear. It was just going to be okay.

The event was in sharp contrast to the elegant banquet Sam had attended in California last spring. The atmosphere in the Gardens was very relaxed.

As Sam looked around the room, he saw his classmates through the eyes of the adult he had become. Each one was on a journey — one they were expected to create for themselves. Each one eager to share their accomplishments, their status with old friends — and that's why Dave was reluctant to come.

Some faces were missing. They had either passed away from a car crash, ended up incarcerated, or chosen not to come. Sam thought about what he'd see at the next reunion and the next.....loss of energy, desire, purpose. Sam shook his head. *Geez*, Sam thought and trying to snap his mind out of the spiraling thoughts about aging. But it was hard. As he looked around the room it was obvious, they weren't exactly kids anymore. It had been fifteen years since he'd seen most of them. Of course, he'd heard rumors which ended up being confirmed, denied, or laughed about before the night was over.

Like everyone else, Sam, Dave and Noah sat down at a table with the friends that we had hung around with in high school. When we sat down at a table with Alex and Marty, Sam smiled a bit because Alex was wearing his three-piece suit — his status symbol — still trying to mask the self-doubt that was hiding in his heart

Throughout the evening Sam heard about many journeys — each one a series of fragile but proud moments. All except Marty — the boy Sam's basketball team had initiated into the Varsity Basketball Team by stranding him in the warehouse.

The air between Sam and Marty, even after all this time, was still somewhat uncomfortable. But after a few awkward moments, even Marty told his journey. He told of his farm in Indiana, the pine trees he had planted, the lake he had dug and the log cabin he had refurbished. As he described his place, Dave looked at Sam and Sam looked at Dave wondering about the cabin in Indiana they had stayed in.

But then Marty told them about his accident that happened on a beautiful day in May as he was mowing the grass around his lake. His 2000-pound highboy tractor reared up and threw him to the ground, trapping him beneath its weight. As he recounted the event, chills ran up Sam's spine.

Marty's right foot got lodged on the tractor hydraulic lever as he tried to jump from the tumbling tractor. He landed head first on a slight incline with his leg rolled up behind his right ear. The entire tractor was on top of his lower back and his left arm was pinned beneath his chest keeping him from drawing a complete breath. That's how he laid for nearly 4 hours. Miraculously, he was still alive when his wife found him.

Marty's subsequent rehabilitation challenged his grit and determination to regenerate the use of his legs. The falcon was circling. He stayed in intensive care for four weeks before going to a private hospital room for a week. From there, he was transferred to a long-term rehabilitation hospital for another month. Finally, he was discharged from the hospital in a wheelchair with home health aides and nurses lined up to attend to his needs for another three months. He was still looking for hope.

It was obvious that through his rehabilitation period, Marty used every shred of adaptability that he had in his soul. He described many small wins along the way — each one strengthening him a little more each day. The compression injury to his lower back created such significant nerve damage in his legs that he had little feeling in his legs and feet. Yet, regardless or maybe in spite of it, he managed to walk again. *So, Marty wins*, Sam thought, *for the most courageous story in the whole room. His grit had kept the falcon at bay.*

As Marty told the story of his rehabilitation, he acknowledged the struggle he had with his thoughts — would he ever be strong enough again, have a purpose again, find peace again, be able to look at the lake in the same way again. He said four things kept him going: a lot of self-talk to cope with his frustration; focusing each day on small steps forward; faith in his Higher Power; and getting the support from his family and friends. Sam marveled at his emotional and mental fortitude to face uncertainty.

On the way home, Dave and Sam talked about Marty's story. "Could the cabin we stayed in possibly be his?" Dave asked.

"I'm sure there are a lot of places like that in the country," Sam replied. "But I'm going to find out."

Then Sam asked Dave about Tommy and Brian, the two boys that are temporarily in his care. Dave said the agency was still looking for them a permanent home and asked Sam if he had ever considered doing something like that. After no immediate response, Dave continued, "I just can't take any more kids or I would."

"Dave, that's a big ask! Let me think about it and talk to Jane." Immediately, an image of the red-tailed hawk feather lying beside Jessie's urn popped into Sam's mind.

Chapter 25: Icy Patches

At the reunion, Sam had run into Holly. "It's a good thing I didn't bring Jane," he whispered to Dave. Of course, Dave laughed under his breath and walked away from Sam leaving the door wide open for Holly to approach. It was tough because Sam hadn't seen her since the break up.

"Sam, it's good to see you," Holly said. "I hope you and your family are well."

"We are, Holly," Sam replied. "It's good to see you too. Is your husband here?"

"No. That ended a few years ago," she replied.

"Too bad. I hope you are happy. Where are you living and working?"

"I moved back to Cincinnati after the divorce. My grandparents had died so there wasn't anything left for me in Toledo. I'm working at P & G as a marketing analyst."

"That's very interesting. Did you finish college?"

"Yeah, I sort of picked up where I left off at UC. Fortunately, they accepted my first two years of credits. Is your wife here?"

"No, she's home with our daughter, Susie. I came with Dave and Noah."

"Oh, where are they? I'd love to see them too," she replied. And with that, we headed toward the tables.

Sam's Holly story is bittersweet. The first time he saw Holly was when his family moved into Covington. She was riding a bike on the street. Throughout his childhood and high school, Sam was smitten with Holly.

Even in college, they were able to stay close till she dropped out to take a job in Toledo, Ohio where her grandparents lived. Even though there was distance between them and busy lives, they managed to keep a relationship going.

Sam decided to take a year off college between his sophomore and junior years to work with juveniles who had been placed in the detention center in Columbus, Ohio. It was affiliated with a research project at Ohio State University and Sam was happy to get the experience. On the other hand, it was Holly that made his life exciting at that time, so when he got a chance to be two hours closer to her, he took it.

Once, they had planned to hook-up on a Thursday night in mid-February. Sam had to be at a meeting till 4:00 pm in Columbus, but he scooted out of it as quickly as he could. He wanted to get on the road to Toledo. The forecast was calling for snow in Northern Ohio so he knew the 2-hour trip could get dicey. He didn't care, though. He was not going to miss this opportunity.

It had started to snow when Sam was on the road about an hour and the temperature was dropping. He just didn't realize how icy the roads had become. As he approached the exit where they were to meet, his car hit a patch of ice and went sliding and then turning till it eventually stopped headed in the wrong direction in the Eastbound lane of I-280.

The 80,000-pound semi-truck came barreling toward him. In those seconds before his car was hit, Sam's fragile existence became ever so apparent to him—the reality of life and death surrounded him. The semi knocked his car back across the median in line with oncoming traffic on Westbound I-280. Miraculously, the ice that had caused the initial slide and the long hood of his car ended up saving his life. When the semi hit him, it wrinkled the hood up to the windshield and then slid his car like a hockey puck across an icy skating rink. Fortunately, he was not seriously hurt.

What was far more hurtful was the break-up with Holly that following weekend. The break-up created so much emotional turmoil inside Sam that it felt like he had encountered another icy path. He started spinning out of control. Holly and Sam had been together for a long time so breaking up totally hijacked Sam's amygdala, the part of the brain in control of memories and emotion.

Sam's childhood had been splattered with a sense of abandonment and the breakup with Holly brought all those old emotions to the surface. Sam's mother's inability to share the truth about his dad left Sam in the dark about who his dad was, where he was, or why he left them. It made Sam so angry, a kind of anger that lies deep and hidden until something happens to dredge it all up. And when Holly broke up with him, it was one of those times.

When Holly left, Sam was hurt, angry, sad — emotions mixing and spinning him out of control. It created so much internal confusion about himself, his relationships with others, and his relationship with the career he had chosen that he was left in despair — face-to-face with a major life depression — another semi-truck. It drained Sam of the energy to get up and try again. The falcon had him by the throat and at one point it looked like the falcon was going to carry him away. Sam was floundering. Then, Jessie reached out to Sam and encouraged him to seek professional help.

Sam's therapy took up where Jessie had left off. His therapist helped him understand cognitive distortion – not from an academic level but from a very personal one. His thought distortions were based on feelings of abandonment leftover from his childhood.

Working through the hidden anger and abandonment issues was one of the most important things Sam had ever done. It took patience and support from a lot of good friends and family to help him get through it, but he did.

As a result of therapy, Sam decided to return to college and pursue a career in developmental psychology to help children deal with anguish and pain.

Before Sam left the reunion, Holly approached him again. "Sam, I wish we could have coffee sometime," she said.

Fortunately, Dave was nearby and like Dave, without hesitation or restraint, he blurted out, "I don't think Jane would like that."

"Well, Holly, I have to agree with Dave on this one. Jane would not like it. Too much history, I'm afraid." Dave and Sam walked away from Holly, but honestly, deep down in Sam's soul, he wanted to see her again. But it was a place he would not go.

When Sam got home from the high school reunion, he told Jane about Dave's question. It wasn't the first time they had talked about Tommy and Brian. Sam had mentioned them the day they all spread Jessie's ashes.

"What do you think? Should we consider it? Maybe have them over for a weekend?" Sam asked.

"Sam, that's a really big ask," Jane replied. "How can we project how it would affect Susan or, in fact, our family?"

"Dave and Debbie have managed to take in children and he doesn't make nearly as much money as I do. Their home is always so full of love," Sam responded.

"I'm willing to have them here one weekend, but I'm not promising anything!"

"Neither am I."

Not long after that conversation, Sam was cleaning out his backpack and ran across the brochure from the nature preserve where Dave and he had spent the long weekend last summer. The brochure cover had a picture of the the cabin nestled within the pine forest. Susie, as Sam called her, saw the brochure and asked, "What's that Daddy?"

"It's a brochure about a place that I visited with Uncle Dave and it had lots of pine trees." Sam flipped it open to the picture of the pine grove, "See this picture. The brochure says that pine trees do not have the long taproot to keep it grounded like other trees do. Therefore, it's more likely to turn over in high winds. That's why they are often planted in groves. Each tree's strength when connected to others enables the grove to withstand environmental adversities like beetles, drought, erosion, wind gusts, and nutrient-depleted soil." Sam was very intrigued but Susie had since found something else to catch her attention.

The passage prompted Sam to have a sobering thought about Susie's future. *I want her to have the root system of a maple tree instead of a pine tree – that grounding taproot that keeps her on track, with strong character, and goals for her future. Our home is the most important influence for her social, emotional and cognitive development. I wonder about Tommy and Brian. Who or what will nurture them?*

Sam's musings about the root systems of trees prompted him to call Dave that evening to ask about the process for having Tommy and Brian visit for a weekend. "We are considering our home as their permanent placement," Sam concluded.

"I'm not surprised," responded Dave. "I could see it in your eyes the day we spread Jessie's ashes."

"Dave, where would my life be without Jessie? Or you for that matter? I have to look at giving some of that back."

They came the following weekend and stayed for five days.

Chapter 26: Giving Back

"You'll never believe this," said Dave on the other end of the telephone.

"What?"

"It was Marty's place!"

"No kidding. Isn't that something?"

"It turns out that his accident limited his ability to keep it up so he and his wife moved away and turned it into the bed and breakfast/nature preserve. It's managed by a company out of Indianapolis."

"I think I'm going to take the family there sometime soon," Sam said. "We'd like for your family to join us."

"I think that would be awesome. We could take tents for the kids and we could stay in the cabin."

"I like the bed," Dave said in a low, dry tone humorous enough to elicit a chuckle.

"I'll see to it," Sam said through his laughter.

Sam called the next day and booked a long weekend during the kids Spring Break.

When the day of their trip arrived, the two families packed cars and headed toward Marty's nature preserve. They were loaded down with tents, food, games, hiking gear, and swimming toys. The adults made it clear to the kids that children would have tents to sleep in but that the adults—at least the mothers—would be staying in the cabin. The children had no problem with that.

When they got there, everyone pitched in to set up the tents underneath the tall pines. The pine needles had created a soft bed where no grass grew and worked beautifully for pitching the tents. A firepit was close by for cooking and just sitting by the fire. The women had unpacked and organized things for our four-day stay.

Dave and Sam had gone to get the small tractor and wagon from the barn on the property. They thought it would be a fun ride for the kids. As they were approaching the campsite, they heard Brian yelling, "You gotta see this!"

Immediately, Sam thought someone had cut off a finger or caught something on fire. *But maybe they've found it,* he thought.

Sam hopped off the wagon bed and started running. Sam could get there faster off the wagon; Dave was a very cautious driver.

Sam could see the kids gathered around something but he couldn't tell what it was. The women had come out of the house and gathered with the kids. "It's a box, I think," Sam heard Brian say. Sam yelled, "Wait for us!"

Dave parked the tractor and sauntered over to where we were standing. Dave never got in a hurry. "What is it?" he asked.

"Well, we don't know. It looks like a lid with a handle — maybe some kind of box." Jane replied.

Brian chimed in, "Do you think we should dig it up?"

"What do you think, Sam?" Dave asked.

"Let's think about it. It was obviously buried for a reason. It could be ashes from a dead animal or person," Sam said hoping to get the response he got.

"Eeewww!" Susie cried out.

Then the kids piped in with all the things it could be. "It's a time capsule!" Jimmy, Dave's oldest boy, said.

"It's a gift of food for campers," said his daughter, Mary.

"I think we should wait till after supper to find out. Let's leave it alone till after we eat," Sam suggested.

"I'm not going to sleep in that tent if it's somebody's ashes," said Susie. That's when Sam knew it was time to open it up.

"Go get the shovel from the shed," Sam said to Brian. When he returned, Sam let Tommy and Brian take turns digging the box. It was an old cookie tin from a cookie store in Columbus, Ohio.

"Go ahead and open it," Sam said. Jane came over to stand by me. Brian struggled to get the lid off but with Tommy's help they finally made it.

"It's a feather and some papers," Brian said, a little disappointed. I think he was hoping to find ashes so he could harass Susie.

"What are the papers?" Sam asked even though he knew full well what they were. Dave and Sam had concocted this plan to tell the kids. They came out prior to the camping trip to plant the box in a conspicuously-hidden place.

Brian opened up the paper and gave the red-tailed hawk feather to Tommy. He glanced over the papers, jumped up and ran to me and Jane to give us a big hug. By that time, Brian had deciphered the adoption papers and joined us along with Susie.

"Do you mean it?" Tommy asked.

Jane chimed in, "Of course we do! You two will complete our family. Susie thinks so, too. Don't' you Susie?"

"Yes! I want brothers," she said with a big grin.

Jane continued, "Because of you guys, our home will be full of talking, laughing and loving! We want you boys to be part of our family from now on. What do think? "

Tommy looked at Brian and said "Can we?"

Brian had a frown on his face and shook his head "no." Then he jumped on Tommy and wrestled him to the ground in the pine needles. Brian had Tommy pinned down and said, "Of course it's okay. Brian just doesn't want to leave Dave's."

"Dave and his family will always be with us," Sam reassured them. Of course, Dave (and Debbie too) was grinning from ear to ear both at being loved by Brian but also at the thought of the continued friendship.

"Why the feather?" Brian asked.

That's when Dave and Sam called them over to the fire. The women started cooking some hot dogs on the grill while the kids, Dave and Sam told them stories about feathers across time, starting with the meaning of the red-tailed hawk.

Epilogue: Outwitting the Falcon

Across these stories, a central theme emerges: our reactions, our attitudes, our emotions stem from perception and perception can create cognitive distortion — misguided thoughts. Our perceptions are formed based on the sensory outcomes — what we saw, heard, and felt — during childhood. That is, the falcon often lives in our own head. When we understand, forgive, and let go of some of the hurt of our childhood, we can more accurately perceive and respond to the world around us. That is called cognitive restructuring, a helpful tool for navigating life as an adult, especially when you've had early traumatic or chronic stressors in your life.

Thoughts have a tendency to run wild like an unbridled horse — kind of like Sam's did when Holly broke up with him. When we learn to bridle our thoughts, we can live more successfully with others. When we control our thoughts, we are better equipped to manage our emotions: anger, sadness, fear, contempt, disgust, trust, shame, envy, love, and joy to name a few. Sam's misunderstood and unresolved feelings of abandonment (and all the emotions that went with it) from his childhood spun him totally out of control.

It is hard to go through life without ever facing overwhelming challenges, defining moments, or catastrophic events. These are the times when thought control is so important because it is when time seems to warp — our reality seems obscure.

Technological advances that change your way of doing things, a shift change at work, the uncertainty of a financial market, beginning a new relationship or leaving one—all these reflect changes to our lifestyle and they require our adaptation to them—our willingness to adjust our way of thinking or doing things. To be able to do this, we must be open to the amount of time it might take to allow ourselves to change.

Our capacity for flexibility and adaptability is a valuable trait. Employers look for it in candidates; it makes for better relationships, and we must have it when catastrophe strikes, as Marty found out recovering from the tractor accident.

When time warps for you, here are a few tricks to prevent the falcon from carrying you away:

Find your **courage**, your perseverance and grit as Amelia did. Courage is more than having no fear. It is having the strength to face our fears and develop methods to overcome them. Managing your thoughts is part of fear management, because fear often stems from irrational thoughts. Having the courage to accept failure and see it as a form of helpful feedback reflects resilience. It can lead to continuous improvement. It requires us to recognize our own abilities—our strengths and our limitations—and, as Marty did, adapt when those abilities change.

We must establish connection with people and places yet find the strength to be independent. And we must be willing to face the consequences of our own actions.

Sometimes it means **reframing your story**. Sometimes it takes courage to face your past. Perhaps your home was not perfect; few are. Maybe your parents were divorced when you were young; or they argued so much that you wished they had been. Perhaps, like Alex, you experienced the shame of having your father end up spending the night in the county jail. Maybe like Noah you didn't have enough food to eat or were afraid for your family's safety. If you did, then you are a survivor and you should take pride in it! Take heart in knowing that you can draw upon your innate capacity for resilience and fortitude to reframe your story. You cannot change your history, but you can look at it differently as memories to be packed away — not allowing it to determine how you feel and think today as an adult.

Dave was not a college-educated man but he had a **wisdom** that had come from watching, listening, synthesizing, and learning. Listen to the wisdom within you. You've likely gathered a lot of it since birth. Living in the moment and allowing your mind to be quiet, gets you in touch with that wisdom. It will strengthen your will to keep striving.

Don't compare yourself to others. We are all different and unique pieces of life's gigantic puzzle. Learn to appreciate who you are –regardless of how tall, how heavy, how pretty, how smart. Accept the value of yourself - your worth - your dignity. **Self-worth** is more than how much money or education you have amassed. Sam saw the struggle with that in both Dave and Alex. Acknowledge your humanity — it is "worth" a fortune.

Understand that after every big setback is an even bigger transformation. If you have a **growth mindset**, you will continue to hone your skills, attitudes, and behaviors. Your abilities are not fixed. Perseverance will most often get you to where you want to go.

Find the **humor** in everything. – laughter is good medicine.

Be prepared for life. Develop the **skills you need to navigate life**, and that starts with learning how to communicate effectively with others. Sometimes that means negotiating when the situation calls for it. Learn how to cope with stress, how to calm down, how to find joy. Know what it means to be adaptable and practice it.

Learn to **regulate your emotions**. Jessie taught Sam how to "decipher" — how to look at the thoughts that elicit uncomfortable emotions that often lead to inappropriate or unhealthy behavior. Scrutinize your thoughts to avoid embarrassment, shame, sadness, depression.

* * * * * *

If catastrophe strikes, what will it be that keeps you going? What will it be that can bring you back to living? That is a question only you can answer — it lies deep within your spirit.

At birth, we were placed on a path we didn't choose, but we can live courageously with pride in the challenges we have faced. We can rejoice in our own resiliency and see ourselves as survivors with dreams worth striving for. And we can acknowledge our strengths not through someone else's eyes, but our own.

It is my hope that you will develop the skills and character you need to live each day in full control of your life, to make peace with your past and live fully and fearlessly in the present. It is also my hope that, "Today, as never before, you can see yourself as someone truly special, someone to respect and believe in, someone to care about and love."[33]

Endnotes

[1] National Oceanic and Atmospheric Association. Retrieved from: https://www.noaa.gov/stories/how-do-snowflakes-form-science-behind-snow

[2] Ibid.

[3] Definition by Merriam-Webster. Retrieved from https://www.merriam-webster.com/dictionary/defining%20moment.

[4] Jon Westenberg. 2017. My Defining Moments, Huffington Post. Retrieved from: http://www.huffingtonpost.com/jon-westenberg/my-defining-moments_b_9128894.html

[6] Centers for Disease Control and Prevention. Adverse Childhood Experiences. Retrieved from: https://www.cdc.gov/violenceprevention/childabuseandneglect/acestudy/index.html

[7] John Roebling Suspension Bridge, The Singing Bridge. Retrieved from: http://www.cincinnati-transit.net/suspension.html

[8] Native Times Editorial Board, April 12, 2015, Native American vs. American Indian: Political correctness dishonors traditional chiefs of old. Retrieved from: http://www.nativetimes.com/index.php/life/commentary/11389-native-american-vs-american-indian-political-correctness-dishonors-traditional-chiefs-of-old

[9] Native America Birds of Myth and Legend. Retrieved from: http://www.native-languages.org/legends-bird.htm

[10] The Order of the Purple Heart. Retrieved from: http://www.purpleheart.org/HistoryOrder.aspx

[11] Retrieved from:
http://naturalhistory.si.edu/onehundredyears/featured_objects/martha2.html

[12] The Dickin Medal – PDSA. Retrieved from:
https://www.pdsa.org.uk/what-we-do/animal-honours/the-dickin-medal

[13] Alderfer, J. (Ed). 2012. National Geographic. Bird Watcher's Bible: A complete treasury. National Geographic Society, Washington, D.C. Page 105.

[14] Retrieved from:
https://www.beautyofbirds.com/homingpigeonhistory.html

[15] Pigeon Control Resource Center. Retrieved from:
http://www.pigeoncontrolresourcecentre.org/html/amazing-pigeon-facts.html.

[16] How to Train a Homing Pigeon to Carry a Message. Animals-mom.me. Retrieved from: http://animals.mom.me/train-homing-pigeon-carry-message-10844.html

[17] Retrieved from: http://www.history.com/topics/1929-stock-market-crash

[18] The International Churchill Society, Retrieved from:
http://www.winstonchurchill.org/support?catid=0&id=1587

[19] History of Street BMX. Retrieved from:
http://www.livestrong.com/article/349790-history-street-bmx/

[20] Retrieved From: http://www.in.gov/dnr/fishwild/3365.htm

[21] The Serpent Tradition. First published by Spencer, J. Journal of American Folklore. Vol 22/1909; later published by the American Folklore Society. Retrieved from:

https://www.jstor.org/stable/534746?seq=6#page_scan_tab_contents

22 Bull's horn used in olden times for fox hunting. See:
http://www.millercountymuseum.org/archives/presidents/091026_06_Wil
liamGCarrenderHorn.jpg

23 Retrieved from: http://www.bigorrin.org/shawnee_kids.htm Bezon
(pronounced bay-zone) is a friendly greeting in the Shawnee language.

24 Retrieved from: http://www.bigorrin.org/shawnee_kids.htm Neahw
(pronounced nay-aw) is "thank you" in the Shawnee language.

25 Instructions for Making dreamcatcher retrieved from:
http://www.nativetech.org/dreamcat/dreminst.html

26 Clay Dillow. Popular Science. How homing Pigeons Find Their Way
Home. February, 2013. Retrieved from:
https://www.popsci.com/science/article/2013-01/geologist-has-probably-
figured-out-how-homing-pigeons-find-their-way-home/

27 Reference to snowflake falling in the preface of this book.

28 Child Trends. Adverse Childhood Experiences. Retrieved from:
https://www.childtrends.org/indicators/adverse-experiences/

29 Mayo Clinic. Stress Management. Retrieved from:
**http://www.mayoclinic.org/healthy-lifestyle/stress-management/in-
depth/stress/art-20046037**

30 Lisa Firestone, PhD. 2017. Psychology Today. *Creating a More Positive
Identity.* Retrieved from:
https://www.psychologytoday.com/blog/compassion-
matters/201703/creating-more-positive-identity

31 Bernard Golden, Psychology Today. Nov 7 2016. The Power of
Emotions to Override Rational Thought. Retrieved from:

https://www.psychologytoday.com/blog/overcoming-destructive-anger/201611/the-power-emotions-override-rational-thought

[32] Edward Cunningham. 1975, The Friend in the Mirror. Hallmark Company, Kansas City, MO.

[33] Ibid.

www.ingramcontent.com/pod-product-compliance
Lightning Source LLC
Chambersburg PA
CBHW071118280326
41935CB00010B/1049